LOSE 200 LBS. THIS WEEKEND

IT'S TIME TO DECLUTTER YOUR LIFE!

LOSE 200 LBS. THIS WEEKEND

by Don Aslett

Edited by Carol Cartaino
Illustrated by Craig LaGory

MARSH CREEK PRESS

Lose 200 Lbs. This Weekend

Published by Marsh Creek Press,
PO Box 700 Pocatello, Idaho 83204
1-888-748-3535; fax 1-208-232-6286.

Distributed by Betterway Books, an
imprint of F&W Publications, Inc.,
1507 Dana Avenue, Cincinnati, Ohio
45207. 1-800-289-0963.

ISBN 0-937750-23-9

Illustrator and designer: Craig LaGory
Editor: Carol Cartaino
Production manager and designer: Tobi Haynes

Library of Congress Cataloging-in-Publication Data

Aslett, Don, 1935-
    Lose 200 lbs. this weekend: it's time to declutter your life! / DonaldAndrew Aslett.
        p.   cm.
    ISBN 0-937750-23-9 (pbk.)
        1. House cleaning. I. Title: Lose 200 pounds this weekend. II. Title.
    TX324.A75828 2000

                                                            00-057866

Also by Don Aslett

**Other books on decluttering
and personal organization:**

Clutter's Last Stand

Not for Packrats Only

Clutter Free! Finally & Forever

The Office Clutter Cure

How to Have a 48-Hour Day

How to Handle 1,000 Things at Once

Other books on home care:

No Time to Clean!

Is There Life After Housework?

The Cleaning Encyclopedia

Don Aslett's Clean in a Minute

Don Aslett's Stainbuster's Bible

Do I Dust or Vacuum First?

How Do I Clean the Moosehead?

Make Your House Do the Housework

Who Says It's a Woman's Job to Clean?

500 Terrific Ideas for Cleaning Everything

Pet Clean-Up Made Easy

Painting Without Fainting

Business books:

How to Have a 48-Hour Day

The Office Clutter Cure

Keeping Work Simple (with Carol Cartaino)

How to be #1 With Your Boss

Everything I Needed to Know About Business
    I Learned in the Barnyard

Speak Up! A Step-by-Step Guide to Powerful
    Public Speeches

For professional cleaners:

Cleaning Up for a Living

The Professional Cleaner's Personal Handbook

How to Upgrade & Motivate Your Cleaning Crews

Construction Cleanup

Acknowledgments

The ideas and clutter "confessions" that come in to me from calls, letters, and visits from my readers are the spice of my life. A most sincere thank you to all of you that I've quoted herein, and the many more not necessarily quoted but thoughtfully absorbed and appreciated. Your wisdom will help many people find a new freedom of spirit, save a lot of marriages and money, and even help save the planet.

A special thank you, too, to Gladys Allen, my friend and oft-times mentor, who provided a dynamite title for this book.

Table of Contents

Introduction

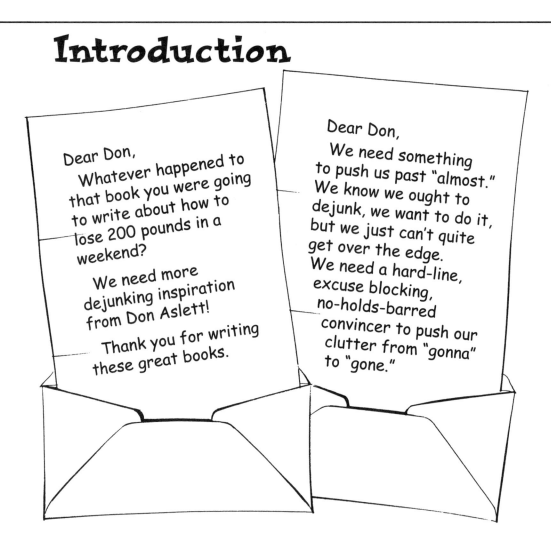

Dear Don,
Whatever happened to that book you were going to write about how to lose 200 pounds in a weekend?

We need more dejunking inspiration from Don Aslett!

Thank you for writing these great books.

Dear Don,
We need something to push us past "almost." We know we ought to dejunk, we want to do it, but we just can't quite get over the edge. We need a hard-line, excuse blocking, no-holds-barred convincer to push our clutter from "gonna" to "gone."

What, another clutter book? Yes, and a much-needed one, too!

I'm the world's expert on this subject, the "too much" that burdens all of our lives—junk and clutter.

You may remember that I started a cleaning business as a college freshman more than forty years ago now. When I did my first book, the bestseller *Is There Life After Housework?,* I showed readers how to save 75 percent of the time they spent cleaning. I also discovered that almost half of cleaning is caused by, or directly related to, junk and clutter.

I got so many letters and calls about the third chapter of *Is There Life After Housework?,* which helped people identify and dump junk, that I went on to write *Clutter's Last Stand.* It became a bestseller, too—the bible of the dejunking movement—and one of the books most often checked out of libraries in the US.

The response to it was overwhelming—calls and letters about clutter flooded in and I went on the road doing seminars and media appearances (The Oprah Winfrey Show, Regis & Kathie Lee, Discover, CNN, ABC, CBS, TNN, Lifeline, etc.) in the US, Canada, and abroad.

To satisfy the surge of interest in junk and clutter that followed, I wrote another top-selling book on the subject, a more "hands on" decluttering guide called *Not for Packrats Only,* which attracted many avid readers, too. Then, because my company cleans more than a hundred million square feet of office space a night, and I have worked in and around office buildings all my life, I did a book called *The Office Clutter Cure,* for the many people seriously oppressed by this type of clutter.

Letters, calls, and requests for information about junk and clutter continued to pour in, and I collected a wealth of real-life information on the subject—stories and testimonials, firsthand accounts of clutter cures and disasters, how-to and

how-not-to anecdotes and accounts, from readers—pure gold. I put the best of these, along with some of my own advice, into a book called *Clutter Free: Finally and Forever!*—a book of insight and guidance "straight from the horse's mouth"—from the "confessions" of clutter enthusiasts. Like the earlier books, it sold well here and around the world and was featured by book clubs and other major media.

I had four books on clutter now and forty-five years of experience cleaning it up. Every day and week new "trash and trauma" stories about clutter arrived, ideas and solutions, disaster and salvation accounts, more and better information on coping with and coming to terms with clutter. I knew by now, too (because you kept telling me), that clutter sufferers need regular doses of "dejunking therapy," and it was time for a new decluttering guide.

So here it is, "Don's diet book on clutter." In addition to explaining how to dejunk and showing you many good ways to go about it, *How to Lose 200 Pounds* has two important missions.

It will convince and help you to dejunk NOW. Most clutterers, even if they agree they should dejunk, have a real problem getting started doing it, and then following through. This book will provide the jump start you need to declutter NOW, not next year or "someday."

It also further develops a thread that appears in *Clutter's Last Stand,* to which my readers have responded with overwhelming enthusiasm: **The mental and spiritual aspect of clutter**—how decluttering your possessions and physical surroundings will relieve depression, stress, and anxiety, and make you feel peaceful and free. It will even help you clear mental clutter such as habits you wish you didn't have.

In these pages you will find a simple bottom-line solution for the two giants we are now battling: "too much" and "too busy." There is a clear link between too much clutter and too much to do, and improving the one will automatically improve the other. Lack of time, stress, and lack of space are three of our biggest complaints today, and all of these will be immediately relieved by decluttering.

I've also included a chapter that helps with the always-difficult "sifting and sorting" of things (are they junk, or not?) by condensing what you need to know about each type of clutter onto a stand-alone page that will enable you to see at a glance the perils and pitfalls of this type of clutter.

So you now have it—my newest and best ever book on the subject, guaranteed to make you hate "stuff" more than ever.

Good Losing,

Don Aslett

What you are about to read...

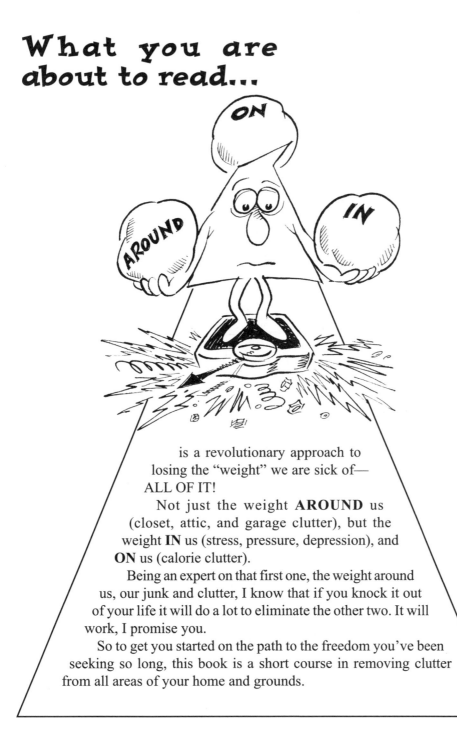

       is a revolutionary approach to losing the "weight" we are sick of—ALL OF IT!

    Not just the weight **AROUND** us (closet, attic, and garage clutter), but the weight **IN** us (stress, pressure, depression), and **ON** us (calorie clutter).

    Being an expert on that first one, the weight around us, our junk and clutter, I know that if you knock it out of your life it will do a lot to eliminate the other two. It will work, I promise you.

    So to get you started on the path to the freedom you've been seeking so long, this book is a short course in removing clutter from all areas of your home and grounds.

Why dejunk?

If you need a reason, let me give you the big one

I was asked once on a major TV talk show, "Why dejunk?" The first and only thing that popped into my head at that moment was "to eliminate mess and disorganization from your life." Later I started a list of reasons to dejunk.

For space, to save time and money, to create a more pleasant environment for ourselves, to cut waste, help care for our planet better, to improve appearance, health, and safety, to be treated better, and for the "carryover" into all the other areas of our lives.

My list of reasons, all very good ones, is still growing. But one reason to unclutter your life emerged as the BIG NUMBER ONE. You dejunk your place and yourself:

To Feel Better!

I know you've heard all kinds of promises and strategies for shedding the "too much" we all suffer from, but I'm only asking you to do one thing that will take care of many.

Think a minute—if you knew doing only one single thing would:

1. Cure depression
2. Up your self-esteem
3. Make you much more efficient
4. Give you more space (physical and emotional) to move
5. Save you money
6. Bring you peace and relaxation
7. Help you become more spiritual
8. Gain the respect and confidence of others
9. Cut your cleaning time 40 percent or more
10. Give you back hours, days, and years worth of time

(And it wouldn't cost you anything.)
Would you do it? That's what this book is about!

April 20, 2000

Dear Don,
I love your books!
... finished reading "How...
... 48-HOUR DAY" ... I th...
... yesterday as I was ru...

Sept. 1, 1997
Dear Mr. ...
... your book: How to have
... have also used Clutter's
... Packrats only. I am

1339 E. Logan
Moberly Mo 65270
July 22, 1998
Dear Mr. Aslett,
I am reading Not For Packrats Only
while recovering from foot surgery. Before the surgery
I de...
I live...

The voices that come out from under clutter.
I get letters and calls every day about the effect of
"stuff" on our stamina, and life. Let me share a few
excerpts here to put you in the mood…

❝I never considered myself to be a packrat, just someone very short of free time for keeping things orderly. But I must admit my house is a disaster area and a source of shame, embarrassment, and even depression for me.❞

❝My mom needs help. A long time ago, we waited and waited to give our pedigreed dog a haircut. She was pretty matted by the time we did get around to it, so badly in fact, that the hair all stuck together, in one piece or pelt as it appeared. It could almost stand up by itself! We still have it, and man, is it ugly!❞

❝I bought a 35-foot long (one-piece) conference table. It was a beautiful thing, must have cost $5,000-$10,000 to build. I had to hire a trailer and truck, and four people, to deliver it to my place of business. I've had it in the warehouse now for five years… will sell for $100.❞

7

" We are just married and recently we moved 6,000 pounds of stuff to our new home, and we have no furniture yet. It was three times what the mover had estimated... "

A man brought a traffic light home, and his wife yelled, "That's enough, get it out of here!" He took it out and traded it for a wagon wheel.

" Aunt Mildred has accumulated about 500 pounds of fabric over the years. She's moved it several times, and now has it stored on a sun porch across from her sewing room. Most of it is in colors too ugly to use. "

" When we went through my aunt's stuff, there was a box of empty scotch tape dispensers (the thin plastic throwaway type). That was bad enough, but when we dug deeper we found another box full of broken, spent scotch tape dispensers. "

" My grandmother saved all the foam meat trays. "

Found in one suburban living room: one stiff deerhide, a cream separator, and sheep shears.

" I can't believe it. I save the Chiquita banana stickers! "

" Gads, I have a goat head in my freezer and 300 hats in my closet. "

" I have 50 years of *National Geographics*. Trouble is, the mice and rats love and have eaten all of the glue on the bindings, so now there are no separate issues, just one giant *National Geographic*. "

One woman accumulated more than 2,000 empty plastic milk jugs, and stored them strung on twine hung from the barn rafters. You never know, you might need them to fill with sand and use for tent pegs.

" Oops, gotta go. My crowded recipe files are calling my name, and the wine bottles I save to make herbal vinegar are fighting in the cupboard corners behind my turntable (and I'm out there piling in more). "

" You asked about the most cluttered professions. I think 'teacher' is the most cluttered profession, especially if they teach art. An associate of mine has almost worn out a shredder shredding old student papers and lesson plans she'd kept. My aunt and uncle are both retired from teaching, so I know. 'CPA' would have to be next. "

" I was hired by a hospital to run a medical office in a rural community. They did warn me that there would be some cleanup work involved. This was an understatement. There were shelves of medical journals in the basement that dated back to 1978. I asked the physicians when was the last time they used them, and their answer was, 'We never use them, we just keep them in case we might need them.' I could go on forever about what I found in the basement.

Upstairs in the physicians' office I found antique instruments in drawers that had not been touched for decades. I found expired drugs which were never used and no one bothered to throw away. Three huge cabinets with all sorts of medical supplies jammed in so tight that when you opened the doors everything fell out. One receptionist had four desktop calendars, one on top of the other, that dated back to the 1980s. Pile after pile of junk mail that 'might come in handy someday.'

The hardest part about the cleanup was believing that this was an actual working doctors' office. There was more, but I don't want to scare anyone away from doctors. "

" Packratism is definitely genetic in nature. In 1992 when my mother had to move from her home, I found flower seeds that my deceased father had saved from the year of my high school graduation in 1967. He stored seeds so well that he'd forget he had them, and so would have to buy new packets the following year.

I, in turn, have inherited the gene from my father, but my need is to own two, three, or four of everything: wooden spoons, knitting needle sets, boxes of Christmas cards, suitcases, backpacks, even cats (we now have ten, but were once up to sixteen). "

What kind of junker are you?

You might be surprised to know there are more than 300 kinds of hummingbirds, and 290,000 kinds of beetles. But junkers are a flourishing family, too. They come in many species and subspecies, variants and types. Which kind of JUNKER are you?

Find yourself—check the categories in the following that seem familiar or fitting. This is just for fun, but be honest!

☐ *Mañana junker*
"It's going… later. Someday I'm to clear off this porch and empty out the attic!"

☐ *"A Home Isn't a Home Without…" junker*
"'Tis better to be stacked than sterile!"

☐ *Wall Liner junker*
"Space is lost if it's not filled, and after all, the average wall is only used about 5 percent of the time."

☐ *Beauty at Any Price junker*
Still has not only all the stuff she actually uses, but every shade of lipstick or nail polish that turned out to be wrong for her, the eyeliner she used back in high school, and one of every style of comb and hairbrush ever made.

☐ *"Gonna Have a Garage Sale" junker*
"The garage may seem a little congested, but that's the stuff I've been saving (since 1961) to have a garage sale."

☐ *Can't Pass a Garage Sale junker*
Hear, see, smell, and stop! The brake pedal overrules the gas pedal here!

☐ *Closet Crammer junker*
No hangers are needed because the clothes are suspended by compression.

☐ *"Maybe It'll Go Away" junker*
Maybe all that stuff will just disintegrate, or biodegrade. Or both.

☐ *"What My Own Place Looks Like Is My Business" junker*
"There's still a tunnel through the middle of the room, and you only have to hunker down a bit to get past all that stuff stacked on the sides. I happen to like obstacle courses."

☐ *Spare Parts junker*
"See that aircraft carrier over there? I bought it from the Navy for next to nothing—for parts."

- *"I've Always Wanted to" junker*
  "If I own the trappings for it, the time to tackle it is surely forthcoming."

- *"When I Retire" junker*
  "What's that? The trapeze I intend to take up when I retire."

- *Catalog Cruiser junker*
  "Just read 'em and reap!"

- *"Reward yourself" junker*
  "Stressed out as we are today, if there's any little thing we can buy to give us a few seconds of happiness, I say go for it."

- *Home in My Purse junker*
  "The doctor says this droop in my right shoulder can be easily corrected, by surgically attaching a 15-pound weight to the other side for a while, to even things out."

- *"Gotta Be Prepared" junker*
  "This harpoon is hard to fit into some of my suitcases, but if the plane ever goes down over the ocean I'll be glad to have it."

- *"I Was There" junker*
  "Behold—a genuine Keep Off the Grass sign from Glacier National Park, a petrified praline candy from New Orleans, and barnacles from Plymouth Rock!"

- *"I Can Afford It" junker*
  "…between that lower credit card interest, and all the money I'm going to save when I stop smoking."

- *"What Junk?" junker*
  "It's an important resource!"

- *"Married to a Packrat" junker*
  "My stuff, of course, is all good stuff."

- *"Don't Know Where It All Came From" junker*
  "I was wondering about that myself, on the way home from the flea market."

- *Early Start junker*
  "Got my early training saving bubble gum wrappers and bottle caps, until I was old enough to move on to Barbie accessories."

- *"I'm a Collector" junker*
  "The minute I get a second one of anything, it starts a new collection."

- *Eclectic junker*
  "I'm very selective… I'll just take this, this, and this…"

- *Live to Shop junker*
  There's only one stopper— death!

- *Ridiculous junker*
  You have it, but you can't explain it.

- *Inheritance junker*
  "Where there's a will there's a way, to save everything that was left for you!"

☐ *After the Divorce junker*
Evidence! Sentiment! Revenge!

☐ *Real Estate junker*
"I don't want all the land in the world, just all that borders me."

☐ *Craft Accumulator junker*
"Cute, cuddly, one of a kind—it's a keeper!"

☐ *Great Buy junker*
"If the price is right, it's right!"

☐ *"It Was 'Free'" junker*
There's a lot of free cheese in a mousetrap, too.

☐ *"My Parents Were Much Worse" junker*
"If you think I'm bad, you should have seen their ball of string."

☐ *"I've Got the Room" junker*
"If you've got it, fill it! What's a few more dozen empty quart jars (even if I never can)."

☐ *"You Name It, I Have It" junker*
He could outfit any expedition, win any scavenger hunt. And he's proud of it.

☐ *Enough Is Never Enough junker*
"Maybe Rubbermaid will start making 100-gallon containers."

☐ *"They Don't Make Them Like This Any More" junker*
"Do you realize this thing is (whatever it is) made of solid cast iron?"

☐ *"It May Be Worth a Lot Someday" junker*
"It's bound to become a collector's item... someday!"

☐ *"I'll Decide Later" junker*
"I'm not sure whether I really need this leaky old air mattress or not, so I'll just set it down with all those other To Be Decided Later's there (as soon as I find a scaffold to reach the top of the pile)."

☐ *Depression Days junker*
Saves *everything,* because you just never know when there might be another Depression. (If it was a BIG enough depression, he could bury all that old worn-out stuff in it and live happily ever after.)

☐ *"I Might Need It Someday" junker*
"There might not be much call for a corset tightener on a day-to-day basis, but you never know... ."

☐ *"I'll Think of a Use for It" junker*
"Don't throw it away, I'll figure out a use for it sometime (and besides, that little doohickey on top is really cute, isn't it?)."

☐ *"Can't Admit I Made a Mistake" junker*
"They do take up a lot of my storage space. But I got them for only $60!"

☐ *"I'm Sentimental" junker*
"That's a maraschino cherry from the first sundae we ever shared, an aphid from my wedding bouquet, and a freeze-

dried pea from the Chicken a La King we served at the reception."

❒ *Evidence junker*
"The way I see it—baby's first step or first time you were ever stood up—if you don't have real hard evidence of it, it didn't happen."

❒ *Tradition junker*
"Everyone in my family has one of these, and I already have one saved for each of my great-grandchildren."

❒ *Clothes Keeper junker*
"I call this wing of the house my walk-around closet."

❒ *Paper Piler junker*
"It may look bad in here, but don't worry, I know where everything is."

❒ *Environmentally Aware junker*
"I certainly don't intend to do anything to exacerbate the national landfill overload."

❒ *Check the Curb junker*
"You wouldn't believe some of the things people throw away. Just last week I found a perfectly good mechanical duck plucker with only one arm missing."

Clutter Health Score Chart

Count up the checks you made and rate yourself below.

0 checks	YOU ARE PURE! Give this book to an overloaded friend.
1-3 checks	You are only mildly infected, but watch it!
3-6 checks	The balance is tipping in the wrong direction!
6-12 checks	You are badly cluttered and contagious—stay home and dejunk!
13-20 checks	You are out of room, and may soon be out of friends.
21-30 checks	It's not too soon to panic.
33 checks and up	You are a lost cause. Start a swap meet or open a junker store.

CHAPTER 1

Too Much!

There comes a day (Maybe it's here? Maybe it's coming soon? Maybe it happened a long time ago?) when your intake takes over. When all that you've bought and brought home catches up with you. You are totally occupied taking things in and taking care of them. First you pay for it all, later organize it, then frantically try to control it. Finally life seems to be down to just fighting it. It's all pure weight **on, in, and all around you.** It's yours, you own it, and you are constantly tending it. Cuss it, or call it anything you like, it is excess, "too much," clutter.

Not only is all this now taking away our happiness and popularity, it's taking up room. It's interesting how the consequence of consuming is the loss of not just our money but our space, physical and mental. Yet how we struggled and paid to get all this, to gain it.

A high standard of luxury, not living

Who told us, promised us, that all of this stuff we've taken in would create a **high standard of living**? Worrying about, fighting, and finagling to pay for the "too much" we now have piled everywhere is not a high standard of living. It's a real case of mislabeling. The only thing we really have here is a high standard of luxury.

A HIGH STANDARD OF LIVING IS:

Freedom
Good health
High self-esteem
Being debt free
A stable family
A satisfying marriage
A high standard of luxury is having all the conveniences and comforts we think will eliminate effort and strain—those gadgets and extras of all kinds they keep coming up with and we keep accumulating.

In the 1980's, for instance, Dick Tracy's old two-way radio wristwatch gave way to hand-held or pocket size electronic devices of all kinds. There wasn't a worry in life not covered by a portable phone, beeper, pager, stereo, radio, camera, exercise device, memory jogger, organizer, laptop computer, calculator, or thesaurus. By the 90's we had mobile message recorders, note recorders, electronic translators, portable shredders, blood pressure monitors, personal protection devices, garage door openers, white noise generators, navigation guidance systems, electronic binoculars, electric key controls and finders. Convenience is often a clutter now, "too much" to manage—we can't even manage the stuff sold to help us manage. We are always fighting complications, and it is really the "too much" that complicates.

Luxury doesn't come without a big price tag and lots of stuff that "sticks" to us. We are now spending much of our time and money trying to recover from or remove the "too much" in, on, and around us. Millions and millions of us are buying every new storage expander or "organizer" device that comes along, books, tapes, seminars, programs, plans, rental storage units, trips to faraway places, pills, and sessions at the shrink. We're doing all this not to live life to its fullest, but to get relief, to be released from or rid of the "too much."

Truly it is pathetic, scary!

We call ourselves consumers but we don't actually consume, we just keep on purchasing and piling.

We have everything!

A successful southern California bank retained me to speak to all their employees once and first took me to dinner at a fancy restaurant with a number of those employees. After dessert, a conversation about eco-nomic conditions ensued. The bank president, exploring my opinions, finally asked me one of those questions we all ask and all have definite ideas on…

"Don, what do you think is wrong with the economy?"

The table went quiet as all the financial geniuses turned to me, Idaho's Businessman of the Year, for a profound answer. I cleared my throat and made some strong remarks about education, labor, government, and attitude in the work force. It was pretty good I thought, but apparently I didn't impress the president.

"No, that isn't it." he said. "What's wrong with the economy is, we have everything. *We have everything!*" he said again, and then proceeded to go around the table where he asked tellers, bank officers, passing waitresses and busboys, etc., questions like "How many micro-waves, televisions, radios, pairs of shoes, tape players, recliners, watches, and automobiles do you own?" He grilled us all on every possible thing one could need or own, and we all had not only one, but most of us more than one. "Don, if people had all the money in the world, what else would they buy…? We have everything."

For the next few months and the whole year following, his comment stayed in the back of my mind and it seemed to apply to most of the situations and problems that cropped up. The negatives didn't come from lack of things or commodities, they came from too much, too many. We were loaded down with tangibles—the shortages we were feeling were in **time, love, attention and affection**, all shorted because we don't have the time or money left over after all we have to tend. The bottom line is, *all the thin people are overweight too*.

A little while after this conversation, a Detroit publicity assistant who was driving me to a television show mentioned that she worked in the malls as a salesperson during the Christmas holidays. "You know, Don," she said, "almost every customer looking for gifts ends up buying something that someone already has. Friends and family have everything, so they have to purchase a duplicate—an updated, different, or deluxe model."

Right she is! My wife and I have six children and we thought we raised them frugally—and none of them are what you would call well-heeled now. This Christmas my wife and I (we consider ourselves creative people) struggled and searched to get them something they don't already have, and generally they had two or three of whatever we came up with.

"What about a watch?" I suggested for one of the grandchildren. That got chuckles. Maybe when you and I were kids we would finally get a watch for high school graduation or often college. Not long ago every kid in junior high had a watch, a few years later, as they became cheap and stylish, kids at sixth-grade graduation didn't need a watch, they had three or four already kicking around their rooms. Ten-dollar digital, TV-character watches that we couldn't even comprehend in the old days, the "less" days.

In the old days the worst of us were held in control somewhat by the one-room cabins, one-room schoolhouses, and houses with no attached garage. But today, many of the new houses going up have three-car garages, and many of the building projects and most booming businesses we see are "storage rentals."

We are now in a time of accelerated acquisition of stuff. It once took years and years. Young married couples now can easily overspend and overown, and charge themselves into total submission to clutter before the age of forty, giving their lives over to owning and caring for too much.

It is almost unbelievable that now (without even a guilty conscience) we pay for a storage unit, a place to keep our runover clutter away from home. If having a jammed, overflowing home is shameful, what would you call renting other space and sheds in overflowing downtown?

Remember the "Lane" hope chest that our sisters or nieces of old had, where they stored all of their trinkets and treasures, napkins and needlework for their future lifetime? Today those cedar containers wouldn't hold a week's worth of our "hope for the future" things. If those beautiful chests had been increased in size proportionate to our stuff, they would be bigger than a doublewide house trailer! There are not a few homes around in which there is so much stuff piled everywhere, in every room of the house, that there is only a path or trail from room to room.

Most of us have been led, swayed, and seduced into tending too much. We set our goals and work a lifetime to get it all, thinking it's a pleasure all the time that we're fighting it.

We hear a lot about youth, marriage, and employment problems, and when you look at what underlies the attitudes and arguments that cause so much trouble here it all boils down to those same two words… TOO MUCH! I constantly see kids pawing through a closet that would fill at least one aisle of the local "mart," whining and whimpering that they have "nothing to wear," lounging around and griping, picking on parents who bought them that too much.

Go to your drawers and closets and you will see the same thing—
TOO MUCH!

Scanning a magazine rack recently, I began to chuckle as I renamed some publications to fit today's reality:
Good Househeaping
Bigger Homes and Gardens
Family Circles

It is not uncommon for people to think their vehicle has been stolen out of a parking lot and then discover that they brought one of their other cars, and forgot… again a case of too much, too many to keep track of. And even the poorest of us are waking up to realize we may be over-housed and over-propertied. Once only the rich could own and buy more land and buildings than they needed; now many of us have "too much house." Banks have some pretty impressive qualifiers or screening devices to determine if a buyer can or should buy a place—if the would-be purchaser can truly afford it. Their formulas and ratios of income to payment are well thought out and tested. Yet when a bank or other lending institution comes back and tells someone he can't or doesn't qualify for financing on a place (it is too much for him to handle), what does he do? He fibs and fudges, stretches and pads his financial statement, hustles up some temporary down payment money from his folks or others, anything to get him in that house. Thus hundreds of thousands of people end up with something that later comes back to haunt them (or they lose it), because they cannot sustain it—it is literally too much for them to tend.

With a strain or loss like this comes additional strains to health and relationships… all for "too much."

You tell me! Isn't our behavior shouting (gasping!) "**TOO MUCH**"?

Look at the:

1. Increase in closet, house, garage, and storage building size.
2. Increase in trash production (we're up to six pounds a day each, now).
3. Increase in installment payments of all kinds.
4. Increase in stress claims and complaints.
5. Increase in trips and vacations, to relieve "burnout."
6. Growing numbers of people retreating to special-rate motels on the weekend, to get away from the home scene—bad!
7. Increase in the number of books, programs, seminars, and treatment facilities for people who have problems with drugs, alcohol, overweight, and depression.

There must be sixty different species of exercise bike now, media advertisements and fairs are filled with them. The racks and aisles of bookstores are crammed, with tens of thousands of diet books. Yet in 1999 studies showed that we "health conscious" Americans are heavier than ever—more than fifty percent of us are overweight, and almost a quarter of us, obese! And as for that "stuff" we own, store, and compul-

sively collect, just take a drive past those homes with three-car garages and see all three cars parked outside in the winter. Or take note of the acres and acres of storage units, or peruse all the new kinds of plastic containers and closet organizers. The big bottom line is simply…

TOO MUCH!

We who aren't entirely bloated yet can count on becoming so, because we are all on the line the banker summed up so well. We not only have everything, we are planning loans and credit line increases, trips and scouting expeditions to get more, to finish burying ourselves.

A day of accelerated acquisition and accumulation

Two modern words that really expand our capacity for more and too much are CONVENIENCE and ACCESS.

As we pass through a day, we are constantly reminded—in the mail, when we go on line, by road signs, in newspapers and magazines, television and radio commercials, and phone solicitations—that all we have to do is touch a button, dial a number, or say "yes," and we can have ownership of almost anything. Everything is convenient, everything is accessible, and the principle of "afford" has been distorted to the point where it no longer means the ability to pay for something, it means the ability to acquire it immediately. With all of the

credit plans and schemes and cards around today, whether we are rich or poor or in between, we can buy almost anything we want, whenever we want. We don't have to save and wait and consider it, we can, in an instant, OWN IT! (And not feel the "bite" of the purchase immediately.)

It is a day of accelerated acquisition and accumulation. The average person has more material things and conveniences, more luxury, security, and comfort, than the wealthy did not long ago.

In this overoffered, overaccessible day even the most positive things that we want, need, and use for pleasure, satisfaction, or our jobs, have almost become a curse. Look at toys, sports and hobby equipment, furniture, and vehicles. They are so easy to buy and own now that all of us, for example, own multiple cameras, usually lying around unused. Just do an audit on your shoes, or your family's shoes! Our kids could leave a pair of shoes at each of four friend's homes and still have some to wear at home.

Has all this made us happy, satisfied? Well, at the time of acquisition things do have some stimulant value, but when the honeymoon is over, the wrapping paper stops rattling, and they join our mounting pile of "too much," they nag us, are expensive, we have no room to store them, and no time to tend them. Our too much begins to hurt instead of help, and most of us find ourselves "stuff shackled."

our midriffs, and too much in our garages, basements, drawers, closets, and rental units.

A flight attendant, looking over my shoulder when I had this little "too much" triangle spread out in front of me, summed up the problem of "too much." She said "Wow, it's the Bermuda Triangle of disfunctionality"!

A sure way to reduce stress

Isn't this a day of increasing stress and strains in families, marriages, jobs, positions, finances? It seems everyone is searching for a way to reduce their stress. Well think how much stress—money, time, emotion—is connected with excess stuff, getting it and looking after it.

A while ago *Reader's Digest* quoted me several times in an article called "Stress Proof Your Home." I received many calls and comments about it later, and most of the people who called said that they had never before associated stress with "stuff."

We have "stuff stress"—so to relieve it, we go out and get more stuff.

Dumping excess stuff is the surest, quickest way to dump stress.

The triangle of too much

We have so many things and comforts these days, yet our level of personal satisfaction and happiness seems to be lower than ever, which doesn't seem to make sense. And the big three we are struggling with are:

1. Mental and emotional stress (clutter in us)
2. Overweight worries and concerns (clutter on us)
3. Our stuff: all of the things and possessions of all kinds we have (the clutter around us)

These three form a triangle, a monster triangle in our lives, a big bottom line of TOO MUCH. We have too much on our minds, too much on

Too much means too busy

We are all battling two big things today:

TOO MUCH, AND TOO BUSY

Our lives have gone past "active" to a dash and a sprint, and getting through a day now is almost a battle. How often at the end of another day at home, work, or even play, do we wonder what we did, why we did it, and where it is taking us. Often we're so rushed we don't remember where we've been or really notice where we are, and we begin to question where we are going. Ninety-five percent of people who evaluate their schedule and their storage areas are waking up to the fact that they are too busy and have too much to tend.

The majority of us are too busy **as a result of too much**. Cut the too much and you'll cut the too busy.

Pretty simple, huh? We can feel good about "much" or "busy" if it is blessing our life. If, on the other hand, it is stressing and straining you to the max, then this weekend is the right time to be bailing out.

> *"Too much" causes much of the "too busy" in life, so in reality we have only one giant in the battle of life to fight and defeat—**too much**.*

The most unique weight loss plan ever!

I've made hundreds of "dejunking" appearances on radio and TV, run many decluttering seminars, answered thousands of letters and questions, and listened to as many phone calls and conversations about

clutter as any breathing soul. I can give you the bottom line of my experiences and observations here in just three words of my own:

EXCESS WILL DEPRESS.

That excess is not going to go away by itself, but this little manual will take care of one or more big loads of it. I wasn't kidding, folks, when I called this book "How to Lose 200 Pounds in a Weekend."

Most of the miracle weight loss books, seminars, programs, and gimmicks are just increasing our load level, taking our money and space without taking an ounce off us. In these pages you will find a quick diet that really works. Ninety percent of us need to, most of us want to, and all of us **CAN** lose that excess in, on, and around us.

The 200-lb. Weekend

All you need is just one weekend to start… and you'll gladly give the next ten toward a glorious finish. Just clear one weekend of everything and anything scheduled (even eating if necessary) and stand in front of and behold all of your STUFF… and begin. Chapters Four and Five will tell you all you need to know about how to go about it. Was there ever a time in your life when the weeds and grass of your lawn got longer and longer, and weekend after weekend went by and you knew you should get at it, but didn't? Then when you

finally did get started, and saw all that ugly old grass go down and the trim, fresh, clean result, you just couldn't be stopped from doing it all, or as much as you could that weekend? I promise that you'll easily lose 200 pounds and more this first weekend— in junk, stress, and even a few pounds if you don't eat those old moldy chocolates that have been stashed under the videos since Christmas. This first weekend will be the jump-start to get your motor running, and once it starts running, it will generate the power and voltage to carry on. If you really give this a good first weekend, any others you need will come naturally… and best of all, you won't be out buying anything more! Go for it!

Why will the 200# plan work?

Thoughts and habits and behavior—be it a bad temper or a big appetite—are not easy to change. Most of us know what is wrong already, we are all too aware of our too muches and don't wants. So having some saintly solutionist come along and tell us to:

Eat less!
Don't get mad
Don't gossip or lie
Don't lust or covet
etc.

seldom makes us change. Few can walk out of a seminar or counselor's office and just **quit** some unpopular habit or behavior. No matter how much they are bothering us, or how badly we want to stop them, habits hang on, don't they! Look at how long and from how many angles we have been working on some of these things, and still are.

I'm proposing the most unique, workable weight loss plan ever. I'm convinced that the majority of the clutter in our minds and even any excess weight we have on our person evolves from what is around us. That #3, our stuff, sires the sorry "**TOO MUCH**" of calorie clutter and mental disarray, too. What we own, nurture and tend, we absorb and become like. An overload of stuff has a direct overload circuit to the body and the brain. So let's use this fact to our advantage, to reverse the process. Instead of starting our fight with the emotional ("Don't eat." "Don't get mad." "Don't have bad thoughts.")... let's start instead with the stuff. We are less attached to it and it is less attached to us. All that stuff around us is easier, much easier to kick out than the stuff in and on us.

There is an amazing discovery you will make here. When you dump a physical or tangible possession, a thing, a piece or part of all that is piled in your place, you experience a tiny taste of freedom, space, and dominion. Remove more and you get more good feelings, a delightful sensation of weightlessness. Then suddenly a sweet, clean spirit of purity will sweep into your character and a sense of control will come to you, a spiritual assurance of "I don't need excess (in, on, or around me) to be happy." And the clean area will start whispering a beautiful song of freedom to you, that will inspire and motivate you to keep going.

The pleasures of being clutter-free will carry over into every area of your life!

"You have given me motivation and direction for putting my office, home, and life in order. One great benefit has already started happening—I'm losing weight! I'm not sitting around eating because I feel over-whelmed, unmotivated, and without direction."
—excerpt from a letter from an ex-clutterer

Here is the angle, folks. Just forget about the brain and body weight right now and go for the "around us" stuff. When it goes (and it can quite easily), it will reduce, quietly and naturally, any problems you may have with what you eat, drink, and think.

So now let me tell you how to come to terms with that too much—explain the whats and whys and whens of decluttering, to gain back some space and lots more.

LET'S LOSE 200 POUNDS THIS WEEKEND!

What is the big "IT" that can completely change your life?

Is there one pill or simple process that will enable us to change our lives, to where and what we really want to be? If there is one magic word, I believe it is "less." By the time you finish this book I think you'll agree. The more of the unnecessary we release, the more of the beautiful we find. If things get ever more complicated and confusing, at home and at work, it is because the whole focus of society is more. The exact opposite of less.

CHAPTER 2

The Many Price Tags of Clutter

"Too much" carries a cumulative price tag, it keeps on adding up as you go along. The more you have around you, the more of your attention, and the more tending time it takes. You might not think you have the energy to work on it right now, but it is working on you. It is weight in the purest, most complete sense. Accumulation seems to always bring frustration, a word you knew the meaning of, but never felt the meaning of until it became part of your daily schedule. You feel cramped, crowded, almost crushed. "Too tight" is the close companion of "too much."

Just what are the costs of clutter?

We all admit that the "too much" around us is inflicting some damage, but just how much? We may not have noticed, because we've gotten used to the labor and frustration of trying to squeeze more into a "no more" space. Or maybe our payment is in such subtle installments that we haven't done an accurate balance sheet on it.

Let's take a look at some of those payments now. What does that "too much" do to us?

It makes us run in circles

The biggest pain of possession is the vicious circles we end up milling in (filling the garage until we are forced to unjunk it, cramming the closet until we finally have to excavate in there). Gadfrey, aren't we the experts at doing all we can to cause a cancer, then doing all we can to cure it?

The strongest and most stable of us end up here—the circle of getting in and getting out. We encourage violence and then support a cause to contain it. We make a law to free us, and then use that freedom to undermine the law. We eat and drink in a way that causes health problems and then spend a fortune to cure them. We risk thirty years of health to get wealth, then in the next thirty years use the wealth to get our health back. We build big houses, loaded with comforts and conveniences, and then spend all our time on the road and in the shops. We pay dearly to possess things and haul them home, and then pay to get rid of them. We junk and clutter ourselves into debt and then take desperate measures to get out.

THE VICIOUS CIRCLE OF CLUTTER:

Getting it, owning it, inventorying it, organizing it, attempting to control it, dumping it… getting it, etc. Such a circle of futility doesn't only wear us out, it weighs us down.

Most if not all of us are in this race, trying to get and own all we can, as fast as we can. We're surrendering some of the finest time and opportunities of our lives right now for the pretty stuff, the glittery stuff (stylish, fashionable, elegant, bigger, better, more). We joke about and shake our heads over our neighbors who are building bigger houses farther up the hill, going for just a little more square footage and altitude for a little more prestige… while most of us are doing exactly the same thing!

We've all seen those headlines: "Families running in overtime." Where, for what? Mostly to sustain stuff. I listened recently to a couple of average people who were summing up their present endeavors and life accomplishments and both agreed that just "making ends meet" occupied every waking hour. Both are a lot more knowledgeable now than when they were young, have a nice family now, and a much greater (in fact considerable) income, but they still aren't getting what they really want because paying for all of the extras they bought consumes them.

Trying to describe her now hectic life one woman said it well, "I always did have a list (of things to do and tend), but today the list is so much longer." She was doing more, but not feeling any more rewarded with life, because most of the "to do today" stuff on her list amounted to caring for, accounting for, and accumulating more stuff.

"Carefree Consumption"
—a lie

Amazing, isn't it, this circle of too much—it's not a good place to be if you want a happy, freer life anytime soon.

It makes us feel hopeless and depressed

I've heard many a packrat say, "Sometimes… I feel I am a "lost cause."

No, you aren't a lost cause, I think there is a misspelling here… Lo… st… is better spelled… Lo… loaded.

I believe this "lost" sensation is largely caused by trying to squeeze good things out of artificial things, or looking for love in all the "lots" places. So we buy more, travel more, own more, accumulate more… gadgets, machines, collectibles, knickknacks, furnishings… yet we cannot seem to find what we're looking for here anywhere. This is where the lost feelings originate—the cause is the stuff—that "too much."

Struggling to maintain a high moral profile and our productiveness has its obstacles enough in life, but handicapped with any heaviness or excess, such as stuff you don't really need, want, or like (but you possess) will give you a real feeling of hopelessness.

Kathryn Hepburn (86 years of wisdom) had a great line in one of her later movies, "The problem isn't getting it... it's wanting it after you get it!"

Makes us "FIGHT" all the time

I've noticed, among the thousands of people I've known or worked with in business, family, or the community, that the most unhappy and unsuccessful people always seem to be battling something. Just listen to their conversation—every day is a fight, with their spouse, their neighbors, their weight, their competitors, the cockroaches, the cleaning, and so on. And more and more I hear people battling with their stuff. You know what I mean, you see and hear this too daily. Folks are fighting to find a place for things, fighting the stuff in their way everywhere, fighting to pay for things they didn't really need. When your hands and feet and brain and energy and space are being used to fight, you have little left over to gain ground. If you've ever wondered what and why you are fighting all the time, it is generally excess, or something caused by excess.

It takes away our freedom

What is it that men and women have hunted, schemed, sacrificed, and yes died for, for thousands of years now? …FREEDOM… We can figure out fast, as life unfolds, that freedom is "IT"—a free country, and freedom in personal choices of all kinds, including ownership. Almost all wars and for that matter person-to-person conflicts, have been over someone losing, or taking freedom away.

Yet how readily we sacrifice our freedom to what that very freedom enables us to get. When people finally get to the point where they are free to make their own choices and no one can shove them around, they let stuff shove them around, and even out of their home and yard. And yes, even out of relationships.

The invisible handcuffs of our 200 pounds

There is a slow and insidious transition here, from when you have things to when they have you. It's terrible to wake up one day and realize that something we think we own, in fact owns us!

As one of my readers noted, "Junk kept me in one place, I couldn't move because I had too much to move."

A man I know walked out of one of those novelty shirt shops the other day with a new T-shirt on. It had a brightly colored American flag on it and in big letters it proclaimed: "HOME OF THE FREE." About the only freedom the fellow had was the right to wear the shirt. He was immobilized by debt (owning too much), and as he himself put it, "I have no time." He had no space in or around his house, either. He had so much in the way of the chance to do any living he had no freedom, and the jailer that had captured and was holding him, was he himself.

We see this all over today—people walking down the aisle of life filling their carts with gadgets and goodies, the carrying and keeping of which will cost them their freedom.

Ironic, isn't it, that the enemy here isn't something wicked or ugly, but "nice things"—shiny, pretty, sensual. Don't we all work toward and fall for the "nicer" stuff, and then when we finally possess it—the best, the nicest—the less we share it, the more protective we get, the higher the insurance fees and the fences and the pitch of our voices looking for it when it is misplaced? And yes, THE LESS WE USE IT. The nicer the home and more perfectly it is proportioned, the less time we spend in it.

It all boils down to... are you living to have or to become?

We've been sold and have bought that living is having, when in fact living is being, and the biggest "being" of all is free... being free... free from the weight of possessions, of things that push us down instead of elevate us. And what are those? The old familiar three, of course—the stuff we carry on and in us, and have stacked around us.

The best things in life are not things!

The time it wastes

"Time" is the prize we are all seeking right now in our lives; we have a hundred times as many things and activities competing for it than in the old days. It isn't a question of serving two masters anymore, it is serving two hundred and we can't do it all and still have anything like a quality life. The best way to zero in on quality and the necessary is to

shed the unnecessary. People trying desperately to "get it together" often start at the wrong end by searching out and adding ever more to their lives, when a much easier and more logical approach is simply eliminating what you don't need.

"We have six children and we home school, so there's plenty for me to do. But after rereading your books, I came to realize that schooling my children, sharing things with my husband, caring for our home, living my life—everything—was actually a sideline; my main occupation was moving clutter around, getting rid of it, trying to manage it somehow. I've devoted my entire life to this project!"

"Too much" doesn't tend itself

"Too much" doesn't tend itself—you don't just "have" anything, even if you are rich and can easily pay for it, or if it was a gift, or you own Acme Storage, Inc. Stuff doesn't just sit there innocently in a drawer, closet, or storage unit. Stuff brings responsibilities, just like having a big family, a lot of land, a big business, or many church or community assignments. More of a truism hasn't been spoken than when someone says… "Boy, this cost me an arm and a leg!" It actually did, because stuff takes arms to care for and carry it all and a leg to run and fetch and stumble over it. The cost of tending isn't all in the physical maintenance, either, it's a personal cost too. Tending kids is okay, they are our life and our heritage, an extension of ourselves. But tending stuff is just "maybe sitting." We hire someone to sit our kids while we are out, but whether we're at home or out, we are sitting our clutter—our family of "too much"—all of the time!

How much time do you lose to clutter?

At least 40 percent of all our home cleaning, care, and maintenance time is spent on junk and clutter—cleaning it, and cleaning around, under, and through it. Not to mention all the time we spend buying it, storing it, moving it around, and pawing through it. It's hard to find love, joy, and edification with your head in a cubbyhole and your hands hunting and rummaging for "something."

Wouldn't it be interesting to have an accurate total of how many years of our life we spend fighting and

tending and handling plain old junk and clutter? I've been on TV with expert "time scientists" who have taken polls and measurements to prove, for example, that we spend 5 years in lines, 3 years in meetings, 6 years eating, 5 years doing house-work, 4 or 5 hours a day watching TV, and so on. I'll bet that if all of the time we devote to clutter were measured, extracting it as necessary from some of these other totals, it would be more than 10 years of our lives.

DEJUNKING WILL MEAN YOU NEVER HAVE TO DIG!

How much of your life are you spending searching for something buried or misplaced, or just some-where in the giant pile? How many times a day do you say "I'll see if I can find it"? Some people seem to spend almost full time thrashing through bags and purses and boxes and drawers of "too much" in their homes and offices. If you dejunk only for the reason of never having to hunt, dig, or even look for something again, that would perform a miracle in your life, be enough of a reason to declutter yourself right now. "Find" is a failure word!

The frustration of "misplaced" can be all but eliminated when there is less clutter around for things to blend into, slip behind, or get buried under. Good stuff buried under bad stuff becomes worthless also—you might as well not own anything.

Ever stop to count up the times people say, "I put it away and forgot I had it"? As one reader noted: "A couple of years ago we were going on vacation, and before we went I hid most of my jewelry to protect it from thieves. I hid it so well in all of my piles that I still haven't found it. And I was worried about thieves—oh boy!"

DEJUNKING WILL INSTANTLY IMPROVE YOUR TIME MANAGEMENT

When you teach or speak on time management these days, most of the audience have already been through several seminars or bestselling books on the subject, complete with secret techniques and shortcuts and catchy acronyms, and few end up managing time any better. As America's #1 expert on the subject, I can tell you that dejunking will do more to improve your "time management" than any other single thing. When you cut the stuff, you cut the time used seeking it out, stockpiling it, insuring it, explaining it, and so on. Little did all those great management geniuses know what truth they were teaching when they advised their students, staff, or clients to run "lean and mean."

De-stress = Dejunk!

There are thousands of de-stressing seminars and therapy sessions going on right now as you read this—stress management, stress analysis, stress control, stress in the family, marriage, and business, teen stress and team stress…. In all of the solutions ranging from coping to cutting out, I've yet to see one that hits the biggest stresser head on.

I think DE-STRESS boils down to one word—DEJUNK! We do have to handle the necessary, okay, but most of us are lugging along hundreds or even thousands of pounds of the unnecessary, all competing for time and space with the necessary.

Most of us aren't disorganized like we think, we are just overloaded with the unnecessary and we know it too, that is what is stressing us.

No matter how ingeniously it's done, all that time and energy expended on overload management is not really a progressive process. Before you know it you are back again to fighting and coping with the strain and disorder of too much stuff, supporting it and paying for it and tending it, insuring and heating and dividing it and moving it and storing it, and visiting it and arguing over it, all this unneeded and unused stuff.

The vocabulary of excess

Just glance through all these words that relate to having "**TOO MUCH**." Isn't there an undercurrent of ugliness and harassment in most of them?

Piles	Heaps
Stacks	Rat's nest
Hoards	Cram

Crush
Overcrowded
Overstuffed
Bulging
Overflowing
Encumbered
Loaded
Laden
Burdened
Haul
Excess baggage
Rummage
Muddle
Confusion
Unsettle
Distract
Disrupt
Complicate
Disorganized
Chaos
Jumble

Mishmash
Upset
Perplexed
Anxious
Overwhelmed
Bewildered
Flustered
Frustrated
Embarrassed
Disturbed
Worried
Mixup
Mess up
Entangle
Millstone
Disarray
Saddle
Balance due
Overdraft
Tax

Too much just mashes and mangles you constantly.

CLUTTER takes our SPACE Too much moved in so slowly, so glamorously, so respectably that we hardly realized our lives were full, let alone too tight. Our brains, book-shelves, and storage bins are over-loaded, and we are all looking with darting glances for a place to put the new and meaningful when it finally pops in front of us. We are like a juice pitcher loaded to the brim with water, and when it is time to add that concentrate for taste and nourish-ment, there is no room, it just runs over the sides and is wasted. All of our space is taken by nonnourishing "stuff."

"Since I moved here ten years ago, I've never un-packed my things because there is no place to put them. Everything I acquired in the past, that is, never mind finding room for any current or future stuff!"

Most of the people I'm meeting and teaching these days who are unhappy with their situation use the word "space" a lot—"I need some space," "I need my space to do my thing," etc. This is another very good reason to lose those 200 pounds. Most of us have finally run out of space, in our credenzas and our clothes closets, our homes and yards. I went to visit a young couple not long ago—they had a huge house with three bedrooms, a full basement, and a three-car garage. They are only in their mid-thirties but their place was full everywhere. It was time for a swing set for the toddlers, and there was actually no room on their big lot for it, because of the grill, the trampo-line, the hot tub, the sun deck, the motor home, the boat, the three lawn mowers, the sports and exercise equipment, all their lawn furniture, and so on.

They couldn't make real use of their own home. They needed space for an important thing and simply didn't have it (and they had a ton of stuff in rented storage, too).

This isn't a unique case. Most of you reading this are in about the same situation. You have no space in your place, or in your emotions. All those things you own and have stacked around you, your stuff—junk and clutter and decorations and doodads and treasures—all of this isn't only crowding your rooms and your surroundings, your body, it is crowding your personality and your mind, too, minding it.

"Out of sight, out of mind?" Wrong. If you have it, it crowds you. Dejunk! Feel the splendor of spaciousness instead of the lag of "loaded"—this weekend!

The question of the century—Why do we live crowded? (By clutter, schedules, habits, people.)

Stuff leads to stuffing

Being a multimillion-mile traveler, I get to see "stuff" in both its noun and verb sense. Nowadays on a plane, for instance, one is allowed two bags (big dudes too, up to 70 pounds each) to be checked and two carry-ons. That is four bags per person, often for just a short trip. People once moved entire households across country in one truck, wagon, or handcart!

Then there is the loading time, and I don't mean for what goes into the baggage compartment. The airlines have added people and trucks and do that, and fast. But loading **inside** the plane has gotten to be a real spectacle. People come down the aisle puffing, and straining—those carry-ons are so big now they're more like drag-alongs. The little storage compartments above the passenger seats in a plane are maybe 12 inches high and on every flight, there are rows of wheezing, grunting, well-dressed, and apparently well-educated people trying to stuff a bulky 24-inch bag into that 12-inch space and they don't quite manage it. Even after looking the situation over, they try it again. But it's like trying to pour a quart of milk into a cup. When the flight attendant (shaking her head in disbelief) offers to take their bag and check it, the person asks if she might be able to stuff the 50-pound carry-on into that 20-pound space. (Maybe she has some kind of magic power that might aid him?) And then, it never fails, the passenger with that too-big bag stands there looking wounded and disgusted because his bag had to be taken away.

This is by far the best entertainment in travel, much better than the movies they play on those airline screens. It is also exactly why so many of us are red-faced and breathless in life, as we try to stuff 30 hours worth of tending too much into 24 hours of living. Traveling light has rewards only a few of us are aware of right now. Too few—the rest are frustrated.

Where do I put this?

Maybe I'm just slowing down and noticing more, but there is available now some of the most beautiful art imaginable.

On the remote Pacific ocean island of Kauai (Hawaii), for example, there are dozens of classy art shops and galleries. I visited one of them the other day and the paintings and sculptures in there left me shaking my head in awe—it raised the hair on my neck just looking at them. Two weeks later, I was speaking at a convention in New Orleans and there was an art shop in the lobby of the hotel. The pieces in there were also so good, I

just stood at the window in disbelief at the detail rendered and the feelings evoked. In the center of it all was a three-foot high bronze statue of a cowboy and horse, in a trail action pose that took me back to my early life experience on the ranch. It was marked down from $2595 to $595, not just a bargain but a steal for an original like this. I had cash in my pocket and could afford it, and I have two big houses worth of space. But bad as I wanted it (and a couple of the other pieces I'd seen recently), it was another case of "too much." I had nowhere to put it—my walls, floors, shelves, table tops, desk tops and everything are exactly like yours. Our lives are so full there is no room for a new opportunity. So I wistfully walked away. Gad, I wanted it, but I was out of room!

I guess if we could turn the need for this book into one big question, it would be: "Where do I put this?" Be it a once-in-a-lifetime treasure or just another one of those "neat things," where is it going to go?

This overload of stuff... how bad is it? Bad enough to make us run out of house space, closet space, drawer space, yard space, rental space, okay... but right now look how many of us are out of wall space, even to hang things.

Clutter makes us inefficient

When we ask ourselves what really promotes productivity in life, the last thing we would credit for it is the constant tending and taking care of stuff. If we would only stop long enough to see how our clutter and the areas where we fail to function well are related, we would be motivated to cut the clutter.

We generally know the how and why and what and when of things... then what is the holdup for doing them? Simple, there is something in the way. We can get a lot more done by getting things that really don't count much out of the way. If there is a bottom-line word for personal efficiency, it is "unobstructed." What an easy way to improve—rather than

having to learn or add a skill, we just do a little removing of that which we are forever having to wait on or skirt around. Clutter makes us zig and zag, and dig and sag.

Don't let anyone tell you that cluttered is creative. Anyone who is cluttered and creative will be twice as creative when they are uncluttered. There is seldom, if ever, control or creativity in the midst of clutter—we are too preoccupied digging. Dejunking isn't just getting rid of some unnecessary objects—it is getting control of your life.

"I am a 'Depression Era' packrat, and a government bureaucrat with the post office. The mess in my office delayed my progress on my dissertation, which led to the loss of the salary of a full-time job, friction with my husband, and bad feelings about myself. Why do we let clutter have the power to complicate our lives to the point of affecting earnings and relationships?"

Clutter makes everything cumbersome

Ever think how the too much in our lives interferes with life itself? I thought of this while checking into a hotel the other day. This little slip of paper was on the bed.

Room 210
1. All entrances but the lobby are locked 24 hours a day. Your room key will allow you access to all entrances.
2. Do safeguard your key. Be sure to leave it with the cashier upon departure. Do not leave it in your room or in the door. Do not give your key to others.
3. For additional security, utilize the deadbolt provided on the room door. This will prevent the door from being opened by a regular room key. As an additional precaution, please secure the safety chain lock.
4. Please remove valuables from your car and put them either in the trunk or in your guest room.

As I watched people scurrying through all the details and rituals of this to protect their valuables, I thought how none of these things are really valuable. The true valuables here are you, your health and mind and your free time, all of which are consumed protecting your unvaluables. What a pleasure it is to travel with no valuables. My $12.95 company logo watch tells perfect time and it can be left on the dresser or in a restroom. It keeps me on time, advertises a little, and if someone rips it off it is a gain for publicity! I seldom lock my house or car—a thief would get tired looking in here for something worth stealing.

Clutter makes it almost impossible to just get up and go. The other day I could only shake my head as I watched our family, friends, and some employees prepare for a short trip, loading coolers of juices, pops, and snacks, gathering up audio tapes, etc., for a trip that would probably be a total of three hours in air-condi-tioned cars, and pass thirty feet from several rest stops on the way. It took hours to assemble and tend this stuff, and seven out of ten of the group were far from undernourished, anyway.

I remember the days when we filled a canvas water bag, hung it on the front fender, and in thirty seconds were on our way, to fish or play. Now we use the fishing and play time to prepare, process, protect, and parade our stuff.

My whole message of minusing ourselves of that 200 pounds can be well illustrated by a common pastime called camping. Camping in its original form (with the Scouts or the family) was simple, affordable, and refreshing, something we all could do. There was a time and places for it, and it didn't take much more than a couple of matches to spark the whole event. This morning, unsolicited, a "camping" catalog came in the mail, all the gear necessary to do camping right. There were 150 pages crammed with small print and pictures of sleeping bags, tents, packs, twenty-two models of trail chairs, mess kits, pallets, coolers, stoves and stove accessories, showers, washbasins, power bars, saws, knives, sandals, hammocks, cushions, and pads, plus 38 different styles of camping shoes and trail shorts to be in style. Unbelievable how camping could spawn such a proliferation of gear. I counted the items and there were 1400 different camping "necessities" in this one catalog. (Not counting the $24,000 Blazer one gets for the purpose, with no money left over for insurance and gas!)

My wife summed it up well: "We have ten times the trappings now and only go camping about one-third as much." Another case where the weight and cost choke out the original purpose. Pathetic, huh?

You cannot travel light with clutter.

Clutter costs us money

Aren't you about tired of spending your hard-earned money on stuff? What are most of us trying to do? Get ahead. Get ahead of what? Interesting to consider that most of our get-ahead endeavors are actually putting us behind.

We often think of our stuff as incidental add-ons that just came along. As if all this were free and we are just keeping it around because it cost nothing. Folks, we aren't in the 1940's with forty acres anymore. This is 2000, and nothing is free to get or free to keep—everything is accounted for by not just purchase price but taxes, interest, insurance, divorces, estates, etc. All the costs of those "harmless, inexpensive" little storage units, those extra garages, or an extra 1000 square feet on a building or yard, to accommodate our overflow will if truly added up, often amount to $500 a month or more. That's $6000 a year and $60,000 in ten years, and in twenty, if this same money were invested and used productively, it could make $250,000 difference in

your assets right now. That's why this weekend is almost too late—the minute you cut clutter, you cut the costs, trust me. A more profitable life will begin to emerge from this first weekend of sense....

We all want to get our money's worth, to get something worth paying for, even people with money to burn still want a good deal. We hate to pay for something that isn't going to serve or satisfy us, yet oddly here we are paying much of our time, space, and emotions, to an actual enemy that we own. We pay for what slows us down, we pay for what shows us up with a sign... "too mucher."

A friend of mine at home shows (owner of a company that makes those small little backyard barns, sort of like overgrown doghouses), said, "You know, Don, I sell lots of these for $1500, and people use them to store $200 worth of junk forever."

Clutter charges a huge interest which compounds continually.

The bottom line of it all keeps coming up. KEEPING COSTS! And need we say who pays?

Junk embarrasses us

An older, very conservative and religious woman I know, while cleaning out an apartment, found a stash of *Playboy* magazines. They were distasteful to her, of course, but a true junker recognizes value. Since they were in mint condition, they were too good to throw out. So she sacked them up to take to the local secondhand store. As she was crossing the street in a crowd where most of the people knew her, the bag gave way under the weight and those slick signatures of uncovered females fanned out across the street. Everyone looked at them, then her, then them....

One way or another, junk will always put you on the spot!

Daily, if not hourly, our too much is paraded in plain view of others and

we continually find ourselves explaining it, justifying it, and apologizing for it.

Our clutter shows on us

I'm not a believer in palmistry reading, psychics, nor the stars, but I do believe that our clutter shows on us. Our closets can be read or charted, our basements, garages, and shelves, and even the inside of our refrigerators. Things like this reveal our habits, tastes, and intentions, how organized we are and how soon we get around to things, and possibly even our love lines and life line! People can read all this like a book.

You can't cover excess with cosmetics, clothes, carports, or curtains—it shows, it loads us down, it hurts, it's ugly. Excess is embarrassing no matter how you look at it.

Clutter sags you just as it sags the shelf.

We all want to be treated better

I think the desire we all have today to "live lighter," to feel better, is only surpassed by one more intense desire—and that is to be treated better. We are breaking our butts to get people to like us better and treat us better, and even the "official experts" in human behavior will agree the urge to be loved and needed is the big bottom line. Again, ironically, a big part of the "too much" we have is the result of our efforts to be wanted and liked. We buy bigger, better, and more, so we will be more attractive. And it reverses on us so subtly we can't see it.

One very big reason (my favorite of all reasons) to declutter, even more important than getting back our space, is TO BE TREATED BETTER.

Fair or unfair, right or wrong, we treat cluttered people unkindly. Even we who are overburdened ourselves treat our fellow overloaders badly. Clutter suggests confusion, disorder, lack of discipline, poor planning, and a situation that is "out of control." Just what do others think of us when we are constantly hunting and digging to find "it" buried in a closet, a desk, a storage compartment? Or scurrying around like big greedy rats, hoarding and boarding a bunch of junk.

People who are carrying too much in, on, and around them are a turnoff—we distrust them, criticize them, and pass them over. Even if we love them, their load makes peace and orderliness hard to come by. What we question, we hold back affection for.

No doubt about it—clutter-free people get treated better, and are better off physically, spiritually, and economically.

Our clutter has invisible speakers mounted every-where: in our front yards and on our porches, in our living rooms and kitchens and offices, the trunks of our cars, our lockers, closets, and drawers. And those speakers trumpet out loud and clear to everyone, "Here comes a disorganized dork— I'm behind, I'm not in control, and I can't make a decision, so go ahead and dump more on me. Don't give me a raise, I can't handle what I've got."

Indecisive you? Maybe not!

Another reason to curtail "too much" is to get your decisiveness back. There is a possibility, a strong possibility, that those of us who feel we suffer indecision as a weakness are wrong. Indecisiveness is not the problem, rather that you simply have "too much" to decide on. Most of the people I know who label themselves "indecisive" are quick to decide on a course when they have only two to twenty choices. When they have two hundred choices they become a vacillating mass of jelly. Isn't this true of all of us?

I've been a licensed paint contractor (been painting professionally) for thirty-five years. Back when the stores and brochures had thirteen basic colors (plus a few shades of

beige), picking colors was easy, fun, and the house looked good afterward. Then selections were improved and we had thirty-three colors. Picking colors took longer and took two people, but the house still looked good afterward. Then marvelous new "colorizing" machines made it easy to provide an array of 332 colors. Picking colors now was a two-trip counseling process, with people nervous about the results, and an exasperated painter, but the house still looked good afterward.

Then the "TOO MUCH" of modern days arrived, with 1,322 (or MORE) colors, and it was pure indecisive agony for everyone (selling, buying, mixing, painting, and deciding how the house looked afterward).

Clothes, cars, computers, tools, furniture, menu items—almost everything today—has multiplied the models and options similarly, and complicated the selection and collection process. But you **can** decide, when you can see over the top. When you have only the things in your closet and toolbox that you really want and use, and only look on the page of the catalog that has what you actually need, you won't be caught up in endless debating and "deciding."

And now an altruistic reason to "DO IT"

Now in the reasons to get rid of the weight in our lives comes the issue of the other guy. For a change let's stop thinking of how our clutter, our depression, or our disarray harms and irritates us, and consider the other people with and around us. What effect does our excess have on those we know and love, how does it affect the quality of **their** lives?

Have you ever considered clutter a severer of relationships, destroyer of friends and family, even jobs? If the ruining of marriages, family relationships, businesses, and clubs could all be traced to its origin, we would often find that it was a focus on excess.

For starters, our condition gives a clear, clear message of how much we cherish "things," and it is often at the expense of those others in our lives, of the time we have to be, share, and enjoy things with them. Overburdened all the time is overbearing, and you can be sure that those loved ones—family members, mate, friends, boss, whomever—may accept it, but most find it uncomfortable or resent it. The space all that clutter takes up around us is not nearly as bad as the space it creates between us and others.

Amazing, how old, old expressions can sum up today's problems. "Where your treasures are, there will your heart be also."

How many times are we called or needed and our junk (and our obligation to it) is so deep people don't know we are there?

An excellent illustration of the persecution of piles was brought to my attention by an editor of one of the nation's largest newspapers. I was escorted to the second floor there once to dejunk an unbelievable desk (at least fifty of the eighty "workstations" in the room had no visible working surface left). He gestured to two of the worst: "It happens time and time again, Don. We get calls for these two fellows and report them not in, because the stuff is piled so high around them we couldn't see them there at the desk."

And what about the example we give to others? Our condition is our example, it is the real impression we give—not what we say, but 100 percent what we **are**.

We will all defend to the death our right to retain whatever we want, as much as we want, for as long as we want. But it isn't really my desk, my drawer, my room, my storage bin, my office. The famous phrase (used by all of us, and at least ten million teenagers a day):

"It's MY life—I can do what I want!" seems so logical and constitutionally correct, but it's not. Believe it or not, like it or not, you are not a single entity in life, but a part of society, of a family, a partnership, a community, a company, a team, a marriage. The weight in, on, and around you is carried and shared by OTHERS, too. "Too much" isn't a purely private issue—our stuff slows up lines, consumes energy and resources, and makes space too tight. This is a "we" life we have here, not a "me" life!

Claiming that your stuff is strictly your problem is like claiming that smoking, stealing, dangerous driving, or an infectious disease is your problem alone. Letting your too much infringe on other amounts to stealing their space and time. Even making people look at your clutter is unfair!

Ownership affects our values

It is truly amazing how our ownership slowly affects our values. A plane I was traveling on once, from Cincinnati to Salt Lake City, was finally loaded—all of the passengers had crammed their things under the seats and into the overstuffed overhead bins. Then, as the departure time came and went, the captain's voice came over the PA system, "We have a little mechanical problem with the aircraft; expect a few minutes delay." Seconds later the entire cabin was filled with smoke and a burning smell. I was a few rows behind First Class, and I saw several of those passengers jump from their seats in panic, fling open the bins, and wrestle to remove their oversize bags and packages. Two big fellows rescued not only their huge backpacks, but their five-foot fishing rods, effectively blocking the aisle, which was now filled with frantic passengers from the rest of the plane.

Others, following suit, rushed for their stuff. Several people behind me yelled, *"Leave your stupid things alone and get off this plane!"* The people who were plugging up our escape exit grasped their treasures and scurried off the plane, delaying more than a hundred other people who could have been burned to death. We shook our heads in disgust and disbelief that saving your stuff could come before saving yourself, and for that matter, the rest of us.

The biggest price tag of "too much"

The biggest price tag of "too much" is its blotting-out power.

Clutter creates an unnoticed layer of insulation—like a callous that can render us insensitive to or unaware of what's going on around us.

The work on the farm where I grew up was hard, and your hands (from handling hay bales, shovel handles, cattle ropes, etc.) soon had a layer of tough calluses. Late one evening in harvest time we were just finishing up with our combine, which had two stacks coming up out of the motor—one a cool air stack, the other an exhaust pipe which was often red hot. Since it was dark and I was tired and careless, I grabbed what I thought was the air pipe to swing down from the platform—but it was the exhaust pipe. I heard my hand sizzle and saw smoke issuing from my palm before the pain made it to my brain. My hand looked black and charred, and I dreaded the thought of a permanently scarred, maybe cupped hand. But the next morning my hand was fine—no pain, no damage. The heat of the pipe hadn't penetrated through the calluses. An amazing testimony to how "insulation" can shield incoming messages. Often the calluses of "too much" and "too busy" keep us from feeling the fine things that are at hand.

Stuff—excess stuff—is the culprit that causes us to miss many of the "now" moments of life. Sometimes the time to do something comes only once. If we don't do it then we are haunted by the feeling that we've lost it. It was going and now it's gone. It

was right there, we were just about to grab it. Then we were distracted for a while (playing with, tending, or taking care of OUR STUFF) and it flashed by and we missed it. It was gone, that moment to love, to say it, feel it, do it, to savor the beauty.

Your extra storage shed is on your property, not just your land, but your emotional property, crowding out your loved ones and some of your capacities to comprehend or consider all that is at hand.

The real price of clutter: Life space, not living room space!

Most of us look at the main evil of clutter as the fact that it takes our room—a simple matter of real estate. But that is not the prime pinch of those piles and heaps. Many of us can afford to get, or already have, the space to clutter forever. You might have four barns and forty acres, two parents' houses, and even free warehouse room to keep your collection of clutter. But be reminded that the floor space isn't the killer—it's the mental and emotional space it takes. Clutter crowds and smothers kindness, romance, commitment, organization, freedom, almost everything.

With clutter we end up tending trivia, instead of our timely needs. The energy and emotion spent to carry along or climb over too much keeps pulling living into a secondary position.

If we used only a quarter of the ingenuity, resources, and rationalizing power that we use to purchase and preserve our stuff, on our health, family, job, or spirituality, we'd all be saints in seconds.

The larger implications of clutter

This clutter issue has bigger implications yet. Something that made a lifetime impression on me, the single thing I remember from Sociology 101 back in college, was our professor asking if we knew the number one, the single biggest problem in our worldwide society. His answer: the coexistence of starvation and plenty. We Americans have our abundance and daily waste of all manner of things while over a billion people—fellow humans—are living in poverty on our planet. This is a sobering reality. While many of us are overfed, cluttered up, and unappreciative, a large portion of the world's population would risk their lives for our crumbs. Six million children die a year around the world from malnutrition, while we with excess waste.

The real ugliness of having and tending "too much" is not only what it does to us individually but the blockage, the curtain it puts up so we cannot see and serve those without. We may say, "When and if I have plenty I'll give to the needy." But "much" muffles charity, not encourages it as you might suppose.

When hurricane Iniki hit the Hawaiian island of Kauai with winds of up to 200 mph, our home (built of concrete) escaped unscathed, but the neighbors' didn't. Whole houses were gone, and there were miles of road with all the telephone poles down across them. Suddenly there was no water, no phones, no television, no electricity—for weeks and months. And stuck up, stingy, selfish, unsociable neighbors suddenly became givers, and sharers—friendly. It was wonderful. But we observed another change in behavior as soon as the poles were all back up, and TV, phones, and good water were restored. The minute they had their much and many back, those same neighbors reverted back to unsociable and selfish. Interesting, but not surprising.

Are you giving up children for clutter?

Lots of young people going to the top, career builders (and clutter accumulators)… end up siring stuff. Instead of having a family they collect and acquire, putting those children off and putting them off, not wanting to have them until they have "everything else." They finally get where they wanted, only to find that now even with all their beautiful "too much," they are barren.

WHAT ABOUT THE KIDS WE HAVE ALREADY?

Abusing children in any way, physically or emotionally, or neglecting them, is the only unforgivable sin

on this earth. When we hear accounts of child starvation and abandonment, most of us feel that if the parents could be located they should be hung by their thumbs in the town square indefinitely. Yet have you ever thought about "too much" as almost an equal unkindness to children?

Having everything is almost as abusive as having nothing. We now are burying our children with too much (too many things and opportunities). They are being emotionally and physically suffocated, maybe more slowly but just as surely as the tiny children who were used to sweep chimneys in England many years ago, with a resulting life expectancy of about twelve years.

Our children now are getting less parenting and more playthings, less personal responsibility and more pleasures. They have more machines and less muscles, confections are overtaking affections. Think on this a minute or two and it will give "too much" new meaning to you!

We can see the "excess express" even in infancy… kids constantly asking for things, buying and getting everything they want, when they want it, and actually being raised up to be junkers. Look at how bad we old duffers are, and we had nothing, or not more than a tenth of what is available to kids today, to start with. Yet look where we are now, cluttered in. Just think of all that is available to newer generations, and with less

discipline, too. How much junk will they have by the time they are thirty, forty, and fifty? It will be horrendous, and will affect their marriages, jobs, and self-esteem. And let's not even try to imagine what size homes and storage units they will need to contain it all. It's a bloated future ahead! This weekend is a good time to change the trend!

What did the most for us as children? It was having less and working more (we all testify to that) and yet, almost 100 percent of us are seeing to it that our kids work less and have more. The exact opposite of what worked well for us!

And now my biggest convincer…

YOU DON'T JUST CARRY IT… IT CARRIES OVER

There is a connection between a grudge and a garage. You have a garage full, you can't seem to rid yourself of it, and it has much the same effect as a grudge you can't get rid of. Both of them punish you every single day. There is a simple, almost infallible principle here: you become what you have, your exposure to and possession of all these things is inhaled into your entire being. All of that stuff around you doesn't just sit there innocently being too much. It silently and swiftly transfers its spirit, its weight to you. We've all seen someone pick up a laugh, an accent, an ability, an attitude, just being around a person or a place for a while. So think of all those negatives of your stuff transferring to you… midnight stacking will influence midnight snacking—keeping for security and eating for security.

Remember the old adage—"First we criticize, then we tolerate, and then embrace" (most of the time despising what we embrace). This is called carryover, and clutter has big-time carryover potential.

Your clutter, all that junk around you, is forming your future. You cannot stop this… except by shedding all those sacks and stacks of over-load… *right now*.

WHY DEJUNK?

TO FEEL BETTER

To stop feeling bogged down, disorganized, depressed, out of control.

TO GET MORE ENJOYMENT OUT OF LIFE

You enjoy life a lot more when you aren't spending all that time digging in storage bins, dusting shelves, and working overtime to pay for stuff you didn't really want and need.

TO BE ABLE TO TRAVEL LIGHT

Clutter takes away our freedom and limits our lifestyle: we can't leave it or stop worrying about it. And if we do travel, it makes it an ordeal rather than a pleasure.

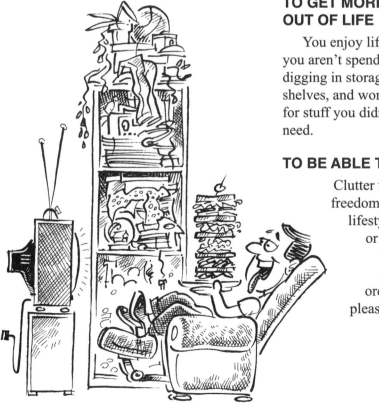

TO THINK MORE CLEARLY

When you're buried in clutter you have no time for yourself, and no chance to think clearly, or to make forward motion on the things that REALLY matter to you.

TO BECOME A MASTER MANAGER

It'll be so much easier to operate after you dejunk that you'll immediately be able to get a lot more done every day. You'll be able to find things when you need them and cleaning will take half the time it did before.

FOR THE IMAGE WE GIVE

Admit it or not, like it or not, we all have an image, and junk and clutter never create a good impression.

FOR BETTER RELATIONSHIPS

No two ways about it, clutter is unsexy, even repulsive, and it gets between us and other people.

FOR SPACE

Aren't we all today, everywhere, feeling crowded, enclosed, short of space?

TO SAVE MONEY

Dejunked people not only tend less, they spend less.

FOR SAFETY'S SAKE

Clutter is the culprit behind many accidents, fires, injuries, and other disasters.

FOR AESTHETICS

No matter how you look at it, clutter is visual pollution. Cluttered = ugly and unattractive.

FOR THE CARRYOVER

Once you get the physical clutter out, you'll be amazed how fast the mental clutter follows.

How about a "research project" for me, Don Aslett?

I wonder what would happen if we did a study comparing people's degree of clutter to their degree of success in life? I don't have documented facts, but in more than thirty years now of observation, and lots of experience in people's homes and businesses, hiring many thousands of people and watching their progress afterward, I have noticed a clear pattern here. For example, look at twenty different people who seem to struggle in life—in their jobs, their marriages, with children, in their money management, with their health, and so on. They seem to be the first to be laid off, to have accidents, or to catch the latest "bug" that is going around. They have more than their share of bad luck all the time, can never afford to travel or do what they want. In general, life seems to be a struggle, all the time. These are good people, often educated and from good families, and yet of this group the majority, say fifteen out of the twenty, will be chronically cluttered people, with overfilled and unkempt homes and yards, and lots of "excess" and clutter in their lives.

On the other hand, take twenty people who seem to be winners in life, to get the breaks, keep healthy, have stable relationships, keep their jobs, have well disciplined kids, and so on. Fifteen out of the twenty will be pretty well junk and clutter free, have orderly, clean homes and cars, etc. I'll concede that education and other factors do play a role in our behavior and in the outcome of our lives, but I'd bet almost anything that the leading reason for disappointing life outcome is **clutter in, on, and around us**. I would really like to see a paper or study done on this. So one or several of you out there, go for it, do the study. Please!

CHAPTER 3

The Big Question: WHEN?

There is one sure thing about clutter… it is not just going to go away by itself. It has never been known to evaporate or dissolve, and very few robbers have ever taken it. And the good fairy with the magic wand is probably at Wal-Mart buying more clutter herself. So what is yours is yours and will remain yours until you take command of it. You've had ownership of it long enough and again, your chances of a fire, another depression making you desperate enough to use it all, or a travelling antique show coming by to buy your cache are so remote, they can't be measured. Your alternative is really some weekend, preferably this one.

WHEN? gets to be a bigger question than Why? What? and How?

The whole force of the word "intention" hinges on that simple word. **When** we intend to do something. We may know why, what, how, and where, but all of these ready-to-go talents and commitments are useless, worthless without a "when."

So the real question is: What can make us shed our clutter NOW?

Remember how stubborn we could be before saying "uncle" as kids? There was some pride or

machismo that would allow another kid to twist our arm or hold our head under the drinking fountain—punish us nigh unto death—and still we would not come out with that "uncle" to get relief. I can recall the biggest, heaviest kid on the block sitting on me, smothering me, squashing me, it actually felt like he was crushing every bone in my body. But he still couldn't get me to say "uncle."

Even as grownups we hate to run up the white flag, to surrender even things that are really hurting us. We don't like to admit that anyone or anything could get the best of us. So instead we let overbearing people—or our overload of clutter—push us to the breaking point. That is the crucial time when, regardless of how unyielding we are, the bone, the back, the bag, the belt, the brain, the being, is going to snap from the "too much."

I wouldn't wait another minute to yell "uncle" to your too much. You will in the end, you know, so why endure any more?

Why do we put off getting rid of things until they start to really punish us? For sure, most of us already know how much harm our clutter is doing us, why we should get rid of it, and where it should go. We already know all this, but it is the big WHEN that is generally the holdback. We are even willing to admit to ourselves and everyone around that we are going to have to correct things, so doesn't it seem odd that we still put it off?

We could declutter ourselves at twenty, thirty, or forty years of age and run in control, confident, and comfortable for the rest of our lives. But too often we choose to keep fighting our excess for the next twenty or thirty years. Then when finally at sixty or seventy we decide to implement the big WHEN, we really regret all those years of "bearing the burden," the procrastination of the when. I guess in the end it comes down to… how fast do you want relief and freedom?

Bear in mind, too, that while you are debating and "trying to find the time" to unload yourself, more is funneling into those piles you are going to purge. The best course for all concerned is to get started THIS weekend. Then you'll have all the rest of your weekends for things that you want to do, not what your overloads let you do. After all, you've often asked yourself, "Who's in charge around here anyway?"

Everyone gets tired of their too much—they hate the weight of it, they hate to have it noticed and commented on, they hate facing it every time they look in their hearts or the mirror, or walk through the garage.

Doing it now will avert problems and disasters

Like the motor oil ads say, "you can pay me now or pay me more later." Dealing with things now gives you more choice than later and will avert many problems and even disasters.

I had a friend who was really into the sport of bow hunting, and his dedication and hours of practice turned him into an expert marksman. In one practice session, he split an arrow, rendering it worthless. Instead of trashing it as he should have, he (like we do with our junk) put it back in the quiver with all the good arrows, to fix or toss out later. Hunting with a bow rather than a gun gives you about one tenth the opportunity to bag game, for thirty times the walking. He hunted hard the entire season, without getting anything even close to a decent shot. On the last day of hunting season, he took his bow with him on a job we were doing in Sun Valley's Sawtooth Mountains. On the way out we rounded a bend and there was a herd of deer right by the roadside, in a little clearing amidst the pines and aspens. I eased the pickup to a silent stop, and my friend, who was riding in the back with his bow, slipped out of the back of the truck. The deer, still in close broad-side range, still hadn't moved. They were three times closer than the targets he regularly bullseyed. He loaded his bow carefully, aimed, and released the arrow. It veered wildly and sank deep into a tree ten feet from the lucky buck he was aiming at.

You guessed it! He'd pulled out the split arrow and thus undid all practice and opportunity. Saved stuff will punish us as we go along and for sure later, too. And we won't get to select the time and circumstances.

> *As one law officer called to an incredibly cluttered, condemned house put it, "This is a time bomb waiting to go off." A little timely attention can head off many coming explosions in life.*

Think of all the time you'll save

In the 1960's I designed and installed landscape sprinkler systems for Sun Valley Resort, and necessarily had quite an inventory of sprinkler parts. The used and replaced parts gradually got mixed in with the new parts—you know how this goes—we plan to sort and separate later. Even though we may have time right then, it just isn't convenient. When it came time to move all this sprinkler gear to our new home in Pocatello, I just loaded it all up, lugged it home, and stuffed it all in a giant storage bin for "later." For years afterward, that big bin took up room and had to be dodged around, and I dreaded the prospect of sorting it every time I needed a good part. But I kept waiting for later.

Finally I was in the position of just plain **having** to go through it, so I sorted through and ended up trashing at least thirty totally worthless sprinkler heads and hose connectors. It only took me thirty minutes, and yet over the past thirty years I'd spent at least twenty hours pawing through the mess looking for good parts mixed with the bad. Later is such a waste of efficiency and life!

Declutter now! The sooner you do it, the more time you'll save. One of my readers pointed out, for example, that the quarterly reports she had to do for her business always took 2 1/2 days… for years. Then she thinned out the papers in her office, dumped the excess and unneeded in files and desks and the like—got rid of the junk. Those reports now take less than a day. If she did quarterly reports four times a year for the next thirty years of her business, that would mean 200 hours—5 whole work-weeks—of free or reclaimed time. Just for removing a bit of excess. When you consider that many of us reading this have less than 300 months left to live, a 70 percent saving of time on one single opera-tion could be a huge force for good in our lives. If we decluttered a dozen other time and space takers, the time saved and quality of life gained would be almost immeasurable. **We could gain two or three whole years of pure free time.** That should be enough to make us launch into our excesses this weekend!

When is the perfect time to do it?

There will never be a perfect moment, a vacant weekend in the bud of inspiration and energy, to dive into those clutter caches. We all have plenty—in fact far too much—to do these days. We have dozens, maybe hundreds of plans and projects, things to fix, things to check out, things to take care of, books to read, books to write, things to invent, visits to make, trips to take. Right now your brain is swimming with want-tos, need-tos, and should-dos. In the reality of everyday life, making a living, taking care of the house and yard, tending our mate, keeping up with the kids, keeping well, and being at least a little bit spiritual, getting down to doing something about that "too much" may seem almost impossible.

But if we wait until every other life pursuit is attended to before we

proceed with a junk diet project, stop for every little setback or interruption, the big WHEN will never come. You don't have to stop living to put your life in order—you can shed those 200 pounds even if your life is in a shambles. In fact often the best time to rid yourself of what is hurting you is when you are hurting. A big secret of the phenomenal people you know is they generally make their whens NOW, this weekend, this evening, this year. "Sometime" is too often lost in time, and as fast as life is going by, it may well be never.

Can you name a time in life when you need extra baggage? Dropping it off and keeping it off is not something to do later in life "when all the busyness has died down." The time to do it is now, during the busy time.

Forget "the ledge"

Often we put off dejunking or push it ahead, telling ourselves that someday a "ledge" will appear that will enable us to do it.

What is that elusive ledge? You and I both have it tucked away in our minds somewhere between hope and desperation. I'll describe mine and yours I'm sure will be just like it: a niche, a space, a time out where I can step off the merry-go-round and pant awhile and process everything. Where I can catch up and get ahead, and then step back into the routine of life and get on with it. All my life I've looked forward to that ledge, that nook I could duck into for a week or month or whatever and tear into all those overdue things. Like maybe when I break a leg and am laid up, or maybe a windfall of money or help will come, and I can stop working and just work on my backlog, catch up on all those calls and letters. Or maybe a new machine will come along to speed things up and give me a ledge somewhere. Maybe during a vacation or outing or on a trip, there will be a stretch of several hours or days to tackle that tremendous overload I have. Believe this or not, when I see a prison movie, I always sigh and think, "Man, if I ever were in there for while, could I catch up!"

Well folks, I've been waiting for at least fifty years now, and that ledge has never appeared. I have a big family and many employees and several companies of my own that you'd think might be a help here, but that ledge has never come, that ledge to duck out of the line of fire for a few days. In fact, just the opposite has happened. The longer I live and the more independent, secure, in control, and responsible I get, the more I have to do. I'm getting busier all the time with bigger and better things.

The only answer is NOW. Today you have the time and ways and means to declutter. Start with what is around you first, and watch how much relief and carryover comes to the "too much" in your head and on your body.

> *NOW is not a miracle, even better, it's magnificent!*
> *NOW is the time, you've already tried waiting and that hasn't worked or lessened the weight. Time doesn't heal clutter, it only multiplies it, makes things more unbearable. Don't waste your time on the trivial while you're young and vibrant. Dejunk now while you have the energy!*

Maybe... (just maybe) it will go away

Aren't we all idealistic enough to nurture the vision, even the slightest chance, that a miracle might come forth, and the next morning we will wake up, undepressed and energetic, our whole place gleaming with no junk at all. We're dreaming, of course, but it would be nice, and even the thought of it offers some relief and comfort. More realistically, we may think we are getting or got away with it, because no one has said anything to us about our clutter recently. Or our junk is buried so deep in mind or under the mattress that it isn't bugging us right now, plus we are building a bigger garage and going to a hypnotist.

If you are still waiting for a miracle on your street, in your storage bin, I'll promise you the wait will be longer and more unrewarding than you can imagine.

Maybe I can get away from it all?

At an airport once I saw a big colorful banner proclaiming "GET AWAY FROM IT ALL!"

The problem here is, once you do

leave the city and all of its abuses and excesses, you arrive at a resort and all the same "all" is there: boutiques, shops, stands, high prices, crowds, souvenirs and more souvenirs, exotic and local junk and stuff of all kinds. One can hardly find the snowy slopes or the stream in the midst of the glamour and glitter of the getaway. And you pay a premium price for anything you acquire, while getting away from it all.

It's amazing how many people think of moving (to a new house or location) as an anticipated solution for excess stuff. Don't count on it— an experienced "weight gainer" can have it all back in a matter of months.

Perhaps a letup as I age? Right?

Given the experience of the years you have already lived with "it," how would **you** be betting? Everything that contributes to the overload around us is only going to increase at runaway proportions from here. Most of us are well beyond having every-thing we really need and still we are offered hourly an ever wider selection of stuff on every side. Day by day there will only be more and better things to buy, and it will be easier to do so.

In the past decade the number of magazines available, for example, has at least doubled, as has the number of mailorder companies and specialty stores. Before long there will prob-ably be hundreds of TV channels and many of them will be cooking, shopping, and infomercial networks, providing us with everything and more in the blink of a screen. Just about everything today can be gotten quickly and easily, incomes are up, and the amount of home space per person has never been greater. All this availability and convenience and all this room only coaxes us into more. No way are any of these clutter sources going to wither away and die.

If you are waiting for the weight to let up, you are going to be let down. The "times" are not suddenly going to release and relieve you, because **more—much more—is coming to add to your too much.** Clutter doesn't retire when you do— it's like yeast, it grows by itself.

Count on it, more is coming and it will double and triple your tonnage. You won't believe the weight you are about to gain. Can you imagine your home's condition after a few more years of gaining pound upon pound every day? Your present ownership speaks for you and it says "you'll take more." The amount of junk you have now is just a hint of the MORE you are going to accumulate.

Remember fellows (you men with overstuffed toolboxes, shops, gun cabi-nets, and all kinds of grownup toys) there is no macho in mucho!

"I'm going to do it later"

This illusion of "later" is a liar that tells us we have plenty of time left. We don't! Our subconscious sense that life is eternal is valid, but when it comes to our mortal time here on earth, that reality is counted in years, or less.

Note the evolution here.

From age one to twelve, a lifetime is forever.

From twelve to eighteen, we can tell it is moving.

From eighteen to thirty-five, it picks up speed.

From thirty-five to sixty, a flash!

At age sixty, we could be gone in the twinkling of an eye, any time now.

In reviewing my agenda for the years ahead a while ago, I suffered a real shock when I divided my remaining time into weeks. Weeks really whiz by for most of us, don't they? Before we know it, it's Monday again. I'm sixty-four and the average lifespan for men now is about seventy-four. That means (honoring the reality of statistics) that I have only 520 weeks left to live and fulfill my intentions. That's scary—not necessarily the fact of being gone, but the thought of all the things I still want to do that may never get done, the prospect of not accomplishing as much as I wanted of the lifetime of expectations I've been accumulating. Our physical accumulation, junk and clutter, is one big blocker of those special things you really want to get done. How much longer do you intend to let it linger, be in the way?

> *"Upon dejunking, I found many unsent greeting cards that were yellowed, or gifts 'to give someday' that were now ruined or outdated."*

The crater of later

Clutter doesn't get any better with time. It breeds and multiplies, simply by being stored, tended, thought about, and talked about. Any plans to lose it later are just promises for its proliferation. Later digs a bigger crater to fill, and then you inevitably will have to face it in the future, a future in which I promise you will be much busier than you are now. You have more time right now than you ever will have. Just ask any retired person (who lived for the day of "no more work," so they could finally get around to everything else they wanted to do). They will testify that they can't figure out how they ever had time to work and raise a family, they are so terribly busy now.

When you feel a strong desire to simplify your life, don't let it slip past until the deadly "later." Ignoring it for "just a little longer" is just setting yourself up for a slow strangulation of your time, space, and emotions.

Junk and clutter just sour by the hour. Waiting just causes things to date, date, date. Each day there is more punishment and less value.

Talk about an argument against "later"—listen to what one New Jersey woman had to say:

"In the bottom of the box, I found a small gold-plated cross about one inch square. It was given to me when I was six years old for good conduct in catechism class. My mom had put the cross away because 'it would mean more to me when I was older.' I pulled it out, grabbed a needle-nose plier, and attached it to a bracelet which I wore to church that day. I was so sorry I hadn't pulled it out decades ago."

Don't dump the job on the next generation

My editor made a comment that really hit me. "Isn't it a shame," she said, "that we have to die to get dejunked" (by someone else who has to go through it all, and face the enormous physical and emotional job of sorting and deciding what to do with our stuff).

How is it possible, intelligent as we are and loving our families as we do, that we have no time in this long span of life to do our own declutter-ing, to control our own possessions. We often have to die first to finally get it done, and then it doesn't benefit us a bit and is a real burden on others, nothing less than a curse to them. We almost cannot leave enough money or property to a friend or family member to compensate them for a large burden of clutter left behind. How

pathetic that dejunking does not become a priority until we have passed on.

None of us plan on leaving the earth until we schedule it and square away everything, of course… when? Someday? Later? On our deathbed? The best time is now. If you have any love or respect for your heirs, don't ask, expect, or force them to go through your stuff after you're gone. A lifetime of your good deeds can be blotted out by one bad deed of expecting others to deal with your "estate" (composed of assorted too much).

Our heirs shouldn't have to face and fight our failure to deal with our own assets or liabilities, shouldn't have to discover some of the very personal things they are going to find, going through all that.

Today is the day to make the resolution: "I will not leave all this for my family to deal with when I'm gone." Deal with it now, this weekend! Don't give anyone the opportunity to hate you for your junk, don't make them lug your legacy around!

Substitute "today" for "someday"

SOMEDAY. You can use this expression as one word, "someday," or two words, "some day," and you can be sure that the bigger the space between the some

and the day, the more stuff will be in the way. The longer you wait, the more crowds in between the some and the day, the further they get separated, and the more likely that *someday will never come.*

You can't take it with you! Anyone counting on that "big attic in the sky" needs to quit counting, it won't be there. Remember, it's dust to dust, ashes to ashes, clutter to parents' or children's place, heaven help us.

I wonder, in our dialogues and conversations through life, what would happen if we were to substitute the word "today" for "someday." Imagine the impact or outcome— wow! Do this with your clutter and it will carry over into your relationships and other parts of your life. Those "someday I'll writes," "someday I'll visits," "someday I'll goes," "someday I'll reads," "someday I'll have that looked ats," "someday I'll changes." The other somedays of your life will be directly influenced by the someday of your junk and clutter.

Why not go for the quick cure?

We've all pondered in some way that future day "when we get the news from the doc." The day he will tell us it's time, we have two or three months or whatever, to go home and get our house in order, to square away our accounts with our family, our friends, and our Creator. For greater ease of exit, wouldn't it be better to get your house in order today, now, and have thirty, forty, or even fifty years left to enjoy freedom from those agonizing accounts?

Why let the piles of the past or present oppress what time is left—be it months, or forty years? When is there a better time to put the problems and burdens of the past behind you, than today?

After years of suffering from the discomfort of headaches, insomnia, back pain, arthritis, ringing in the ears, or whatever, what if someone offered you relief that involved no cost and no drugs—just a few days or a weekend or two of simple activities and it would all go away? How would you react? There's no doubt about it—you wouldn't wait a minute to eliminate those nagging, punishing plagues. Why not do the same for that which is suffocating, distracting, and burdening you—the weight on, in, and around you—your stuff—that ugly EXCESS!

How long are you going to wait to change things?

I get hundreds of "horror" letters from people about the pressures clutter has inflicted on them. Among the most shocking are the newspaper stories sent to me about such things. In 1997 the Orange County California *Register*, for example, carried a cover story about a recluse whose body was found in his junk-filled home. A concerned neighbor waded through the living room to check on him and saw feet sticking out from under a pile of crumbling boxes and ancient magazines. Firefighters had to break out windows to remove junk so they could get to the body.

We may think that being found dead in such circumstances would be shameful, but many of us are **living** in the same basic condition—our clutter just hasn't totally engulfed us yet. We are buried alive, and this is just as, or even more, pathetic.

WHEN is the big question here, WHEN are we going to change things? When they find our feet sticking out from under our pile of millennium collectibles and computer gear? Where will it all end if you don't end it?

Don't wait until junk and clutter are terminal

Clutter doesn't seem to worry us too much as long as we know we have the physical strength and space to handle it. As long as we're convinced we have the upper hand, the zero hour for dejunking can come at any time. But one day we may realize that we are getting older and the junk deeper. It's become like a noxious weed out of control, we just can't hack it out now, it's gained on us. We can't even lift it now, and the friends and relatives we were going to share it with (or dump it on) are fewer and feebler.

Don't wait until you're too weak to win the war on your whatnot collection, until it has the upper hand because your hands have slowed down. Don't wait until junk and clutter are terminal!

One last big reason not to wait

If this isn't a do-it-now-er, what is?

"Dear Don,

Please send my mother any hints you have on how to clear up clutter. She is a genuine packrat and our house is so cluttered I can't have my friends over. I try to help her clean the house but I don't know where to start. I am twelve years old and would like to have my friends over… sometime."

Believe it or not, folks, I get letters like this from kids all the time. Might your children be being cheated out of life too, because you are choosing to live with stuff that crowds them out?

If you can't or won't dejunk for yourself, do it for your children. Your rooms full will educate them more effectively than any classroom, in all the wrong things.

BUT… But What?

"But, I…" Here come the excuses, and we've heard them all, from "As soon as I toss it, I'll need it," to "It was a gift…." "It's handmade…," "It's the last one…," and "I'll find its mate, someday…." I have no end of good excuses for clutter on file, and there are some amazing ones among them, such as:

(The guy who kept a big boxful of combination locks to which he had no combination:)

"My mother-in law is a chronic junker. The next time we go to visit her I'm going to bring along that box of old locks, and tell her I am going to dump them because I can't find the combination. I can just see her now, spinning those dials frantically in hopes of lucking on to the combination and saving them from extinction. Oh, sweet revenge."

(The woman who has a badly warped wood trivet that has ruined ten table tops:)

"Well, I might have a warped pan I need to take to the table someday."

(The man who saves dead batteries:)

"When I get mad at my wife, I go down to the basement and crush them in my vise."

Well maybe, once in a while, an excuse is justified. But **the percentages are against you**.

The #1 excuse for keeping an overkill of stuff, too much, is "I might need it someday." If you extend imagination and applications far enough into the future (like eighty years) that might be an entirely true statement, but what about in the meantime? Even the valuable has a devaluation point, when it crowds and crazes your existence right now.

Like that old car you kept to restore. The family hated it, your wife left you over it, and now restoration of family and marriage is the problem. Or that old motor you hung on to. You kept it and kept it, and it stained the garage floor and skinned your shanks more than once when you stumbled over it. About forty years later, when a use finally came, you had to upgrade that motor to code and the total cost was $30 more than just buying a new one.

Or that cast iron cookstove, "just like Grandma used to use," you bought at a real bargain and dreamed of installing in a rustic cabin in the

Now *That's* a Lame Excuse! Why do you think they make Ladders?

woods some day. Meanwhile, it took up about a quarter of the garage, dented one car door and a fender, and provided a great place for messy families of mice to nest. You had to pay four strong men to help out every time it had to be moved for any reason. By the time you were actually in a position to consider a cabin in the woods, the stove was so badly rusted no fire would dare be made in it, and one leg had given way.

Even if "you need it," keeping it might not pay. A man bought a $170 machine. He kept it for twenty years and only used it once every five. All that time he stored it, and had people asking to borrow it. He could have rented the same machine for $7 when he needed it, and would only have paid a total of about $30 rent over all that time. Plus he wouldn't have to store it, maintain it, try to retrieve it from the people who borrowed it, and so on.

What about that big pile of old shingles you kept, insisting it might come in handy some day? For more than two decades, it took up the space in the shed you really could have used to keep the mower out of the rain and sun. All that time, the pile looked ugly and gave rats and snakes a place to hide. A possible use for the shingles finally surfaces, but you can't use them because you've discovered they're full of asbestos. You can't even find a place to get rid of them now, because no landfill or

garbage pickup service wants them.
It's time to play the percentages.

NOW… THIS WEEK-
END… is the time to do it, an
act that will free many more
weekends.

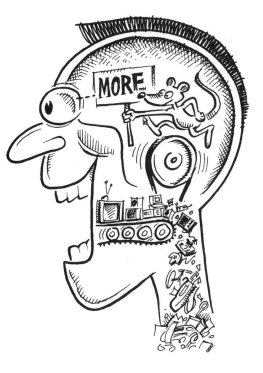

"But my 'weight' problem is serious"

Let's not let this necessary weight losing—200 pounds or 2000—get too complicated. Sometimes a simple problem is made complicated in the solving.

Many people with a clutter problem seek an exotic diagnosis for it, and then go off for counseling, hire a professional dejunker, visit a clinic, join a club, make a public or private confession of it, or file clutteruptcy. We can go off the deep end finding all kinds of genetic and deep psychological reasons for "our problem" when it isn't necessarily so. We may not have a serious case of compulsive Packratism. We may have simply picked up and stored too much, totally normal conduct in our incredibly "over-offered" world. There is no cause to consider institutionalizing yourself over too many shoes or cardboard boxes (with who knows what in them). We aren't talking about a pathological problem here such as chemical dependency. Decluttering is a form of cleaning, some-thing we all understand and can do.

Seldom do we need support… we just need a little simple deporting of things. We need to spend less time focussing on the difference between our right and left brain, and just use our whole brain to clear out the clutter and free ourselves. And when we walk away from the "around" stuff, many of our other problems will walk away from us.

"Own up" to your clutter

Until we quit blaming other people for unloading it on us, or coming forth with "no time" as the reason we're not getting rid of our clutter, we aren't going to get anywhere. I've noticed a parallel to chronic junkers in parents whose kids end up in serious problems. Many a parent's main rationale for their kid's problems is "they got in with the wrong crowd." It's never the kid's fault, it's always that "wrong crowd" that caused the heartaches (note the crowd never gets any credit when the kid exceeds everyone's expectations). As long as your clutter problem is your spouse, your too-small house, the parent who gave it all to you, the company that keeps sending you catalogs, etc., you'll get never get anywhere with your stuff. Ownership is one thing, but taking **full** ownership is the key to conquering clutter. Once the tattered toy duck stops here, you're on your way!

Getting rid of something you just don't want any more is taking control, the ultimate act of ownership!

Now a little reminder of the reasons to get rid of it…

1. Yes, it shows

It speaks for and about you, all the time.

Your junk may be "your business," but it's show and tell when it comes to the public and the rest of your household. There isn't enough storage space or ingenious enough "organizers" to conceal the appearance and effects of clutter. It pops up not just all over your home and yard, your real estate, but in your habits, conversation, thoughts, and emotions, even the notches on your belt. What you have you have, and in a far from indirect way, it is on display every day—everyone notices and judges it and speaks of it (and has to cope with it). It provides plenty of information about you and eventually much embarrassment. Designs and stripes can't hide this obesity in the environment. Everyone knows your label without your wearing it.

We worry about a little weight gain on the hips, but what about the gains in our storage crypts?—ten times as noticeable. All you lean folks who can eat like hogs without gaining an inch, you may have more excess showing than anyone.

2. It's a built-in (always with you) obstacle course

Most of us will acknowledge that indeed you "can't take it with you," when you die, but we're often unaware that we're taking it with us mentally and physically everywhere now, and paying for that poundage. Clutter runs us on an obstacle course and renders us ineffective twenty-four hours of every day we own it—the more stuff the stiffer the course. Every day we have to wrestle with all that, hunt and rummage through it, stumble over it, clean around it, tend, protect, and insure it, wait on it, and worst of all try to explain it to all those folks giving us the eye.

Your junk is the most expensive guest you'll ever put up, and it takes from your life rather than adds to it, as you imagined and intended when you kept it.

3. It's holding you back, and down

Once you're free of all those piles, all that weight, you can at last go after what is whistling past in life. Isn't it frustrating to see so many things to do, places to go, people to love, experiences to cherish, and you are getting little or none of all this because you are locked into the stagnation of your stuff?

Once you're dejunked, too, your seeds can grow. You, like any living thing, have numerous seeds (potentials, dreams, opportunities) inside you. But if there is no room for them to take root and sprout, seeds cannot and will not grow. "Too junked" jams our ambition and creativity. We spend our time floundering rather than in fascinating, productive, growing experiences.

4. You CAN lose it!

For sure it won't go away by itself, and it's cancerous even left in containers.

Fortunately, to fix things here there is nothing you have to buy or join. You just need to do a little shakedown of some of that "too much" you're sick and tired of having around anyway. The great day of dejunking takes no skill or money—just a bit of deciding, digging, and doing. Instant results! (Hopefully this weekend!)

Try a space lift instead of a face lift!

The miracles of modern surgery can offer us all kinds of cosmetic operations and procedures. And surely there is a time and place when a "face lift" might be truly beneficial, to remove sagging or excess skin and erase bumps, bulges, and blemishes. But think of the "doctoring" you and I could do ourselves to make us feel better and make us more attractive, by giving a place lift or space lift to all of that sagging and nagging around us! We have the time, the place, and the credentials to do it, after all, we own all that.

Spending three hours dejunking will beat a three-day self-esteem seminar any day, just try it!

What a wonderful anti-aging agent!

If Ponce De Leon had pounced on his extra stuff instead of searching for that fountain, he would have been a good part of his life ahead. We can't do much about the process of aging, but we can stop doing things that speed up the process. Think for a minute, what has put the most miles on your body and soul—acquiring, organizing, sorting, shuffling, and retrieving stuff! What you drag, lift, carry, and move is what wears you down and out.

How long will it take?

This is the day of instant gratification—fast foods, push-button entertainment, nonstop flights, speedy oil changes, instant answers, one-hour photos, next-day delivery, quick-drying paint. We are almost back to the childhood stage of wanting and expecting everything "Now"—patience and investment and saving and waiting are hardly even part of our thinking process any more. All of

us are getting this way, so don't think you are excused from wanting results RIGHT NOW, not ten years from now. "How fast does it grow?" "How soon will this pill work?" "When will that package get there?" "FAX it, please." We all ask any number of "fast" questions every day, and to answer us, things are faster, almost unbelievably so. Mail that once took months can now be transmitted in minutes, even from overseas! In seconds, we can do mathematical and engineering calculations that took even brilliant people days before.

Yet when it comes to our clutter, this is one time our estimates of how long it will take to do something (get RID of it) go into centuries. But all those piles and heaps, closets and cabinets full! It'll take months, maybe years, to even make a dent in this.

Not so! There is fast disposal, too, and really the only slow part, the part you have to be concerned with, is your commitment or decision to do it. People will be out to your house or lawn almost instantly when you put out the word or the sign, that you are going to give some away.

One weekend will get you a long ways.

Freedom is as close as your calendar. Let's lose the first 200 pounds this week-end.

It always comes back to your personal decision, this 200 pounds.

It is going to be a bigger pair of pants or a smaller waist.

It is going to be a bigger court-yard or less clutter.

It is going to be a bigger head-ache or more head room.

You have to choose. You can use your time to fight stuff, or to forge ahead.

The only magic is now, today.

CHAPTER 4

The Simple Pound-Shedding Solution: Subtraction!

Most people will agree that we need relief from the "too much" here at the beginning of the twenty-first century. The search to find ways to unload all the clutter in, on, and around us is at the very height of intensity. Some of us are almost totally preoccupied with the idea of ridding ourselves of all the weight and pressure we have accumulated.

What can I do?

Where can I go?

Is there anything I can buy?

What can I take?

Who can I consult with?

Where is the program?

There are all kinds of remedies and solutions around today, from PhD's, MBA's, and CEO's. Books, articles, videos, seminars, and advisers are everywhere. Talk shows alone cover every conceivable problem, case, and cure hourly and weekly. University studies, TV special reports, wonder drugs, call-in shows, ministers, neighbors, and relatives have all the answers, and yet look around… **nothing seems to be working too well**.

Too many magazine articles, seminars, and books teach us to handle (cope with) our excess instead of getting rid of it. Expanding our files, closets, hard drive capacity, payments, and facilities to fit it, or storage units to keep it, doesn't do anything for the "IT" and its damage to us. This is just like disguising extra pounds by designing looser clothing to hide them, or wearing a girdle to compress them. Closet organizers, for example, were invented to increase the utility of our closet space, provide greater convenience and accessibility. They have been transformed into compacting units—the closet still contains **TOO MUCH** junk… now it is organized junk, and there is more of it.

> *Think about it. Aren't many of the solutions for **"TOO MUCH"** just tempting us to add more?*

May we be reminded of all the brochures, offers, and advertisements, many of which can be summed up by this one:

Tired? Stressed?
Need Energy?
Try …

The advice always seems to be try, buy, get, add, use—seldom the short solution of **removing the cause** of "tired, stressed, and worn," the unfruitful things that use our energy—all that clutter. The only real option, if you want to conquer and control it, is to lose it, **let it go**, leave some room for the rest of life.

Some simple math will show the way

Interesting how basic the answers to many problems are, and this "too much" problem comes down to simple arithmetic. If we understand and believe in addition, subtraction, multiplication, and division, we have our problem figured out. As long as you continue with addition (buying and getting more and bringing it home), you will end up with more, an increase. With clutter you don't have to know how to multiply because

junk is self-perpetuating—one thing needs another, a matching one, a shelf, an accessory, something to complement it or contrast with it, a tool or two to tend it, and soon what you have added has been multiplied. If you try division—splitting or dividing junk (especially with kids and friends)—you will usually end up with the remainder.

Simple math. It leaves you only one logical alternative… **subtraction**. Now that works—you have five, take away three, and you have two and more room, more peace, etc.

There is no mystery as to what relieves us, it's taking away, subtraction, and the only time is **NOW**!

Let's get started with the area I have the most experience in, the weight around us. Remember I'm betting, even promising, that if you eliminate this stuff you will without much effort lose the clutter in and on you.

What you need to do with those excess objects of all kinds is to **shed** them—and I don't mean move them to the backyard shed either, so don't let your heaping little heart beat too fast. The shed I'm referring to here is discard, eliminate, evict, chuck, ditch, dump, reject, recycle, or scrap them.

Where will you find the time?

We all feel short of time, pressed by "priorities"—we

IN CASE OF **EMERGENCY DEJUNKING** BREAK GLASS!

know we just can't fit anything else in right now. But if we took a hard look at our daily and weekly schedule, we might find that many of the activities tightly squeezed in there don't really count for much. Such as those thirty hours of TV a week, analyzing the Chargers vs. Raiders chances for two hours, and much of the stuff we are reading or running to. Many of these things just drift into our lives like all that stuff did and they do not advance any worthwhile cause. How many times have you missed something that you planned to do, and were all shook up and irritated at the time. Yet later, you realized that by missing it, you really didn't miss anything at all. You were actually glad you missed it!

Let's look at the time you have available for dejunking—it's more than you think.

Take some of your junk tending time

That very same person—you— who just said they had no time to dejunk does somehow oddly have the time, endless time, it seems, to dust, stack, arrange, rearrange, move, and anguish over your junk—not to mention all those expeditions to get more. Put a moratorium on junk tending and junk hunting for a while, till your dejunking is done. Spend those evenings and weekends purging closets and bins instead of reshuffling clutter and cruising the mall. You

could call it a "canning campaign," and it'll save money, too.

Weekends and holidays

A sacrilege to even suggest this? Not really. These precious breaks from our workday routine are meant to stimulate, refresh, and uplift us. But much if not most of what we ordinarily do on weekends and "special days" and holidays is couch-potato, cruise, fight crowds, and complicate our lives in noisy, expensive places. It ends up too much and we end up exhausted, aggravated, and "hung over" in more ways than one. A good solid session of dejunking, on the other hand, is one of the best drug-free highs and cures for depression around.

Independence Day—what a day for dejunking!

Plan a junk-free vacation

When you get your life in order to the point that you could leave on a one-month vacation, then stop. Take the time off from work, but **don't go anywhere**, stay home and dejunk. Dig through all of the "I wonder what's in this" piles, open all the old files and folders, go through every box and bag in your storage, near and far. Many mysteries will be solved, many small burdens will be lifted, and a new life with more freedom will come. You will find many things you thought you had lost, including genius you forgot long ago, and idealism you wrote off over time so it wouldn't hurt (and you know better how to put it in action now).

This stay-home dejunking vacation will end up being the finest of your life, the first real vacation you've ever had. You'll probably be $5000 to the good, too, between what you make selling things you don't care about any more, and what you save in gas, plane fares, hotels, and not going out and about doing and buying things. This could literally be called a junk-free vacation.

Whenever you're weather bound

For most of us, at least three quarters of our clutter is indoor clutter, so we can go after it when other activities have been wiped from the calendar by rain, snow, mud, or flood.

When we have a sudden change in our schedule, or big hunk of unexpected "down time," we too often seem like people in jail: captured, confused, and with no way to escape. Remember that the guys who escape— one out of one

thousand—are the ones who use "the time" to start digging (in this case, in your clutter).

Time fragments

Planning to attack your mass of stuff in one mighty charge is a good way to never start, or at least delay it for another decade. (It will probably have doubled in volume by then.) As the old sage told the overwhelmed hunter, you can indeed eat a whole elephant: one bite at a time.

Our days always have little stretches of fifteen minutes here, ten minutes here, and twenty-five minutes there when we have no choice but to wait around for something. You don't have to just twiddle your

thumbs or cuss the cause of the delay—you can open a drawer (or your briefcase, or a file, or the glove compartment) and do some dejunking. **You don't have to do nothing at all because you can't do a lot.** We're all looking for more time, and those time fragments add up, often to most of a day. USE THEM! Clutter came in little by little, and we can get it out that way, too.

The way steady daily progress adds up is like the miracle of compound interest, or watching a tiny drip of water fill a barrel... overnight! A couple of tosses a day is 700 pieces of clutter gone by this time next year.

I know a man who is quite selective as to what he watches on TV. He owns one of those little remote controls we call "nukers" because at the touch of a button you can eliminate a message or program you don't want. The (hour-long) nightly news starts and he nukes the latest installment of that sensational trial, the impending sports strike, commercials, the pronouncements of some self-serving politician.

Out of a sixty-minute newscast he only watches what he wants, maybe seven and a half minutes. He uses the rest of the time productively—dejunking!

You can MAKE the time

I know we often think we have "no time" to take on a single thing more in our loaded life. But if you want to dejunk badly enough, you can and will make the time to do it. (Just like you make the time to see someone you really want to see, or do anything you really want to do.) When we say we're "too busy" to do something, it usually only means there are other things we want to do more. Once you truly commit and decide to declutter, you will have the time.

Chart your course

Big piles of junk, like a big journey, can be forbidding if you try to tackle them all at once or helter-skelter. Before sailors set out across an ocean, or astronauts take off for Mars, they break the journey down to a "charted course." Likewise, taking that huge looming mass of clutter out of your mind and putting it on paper somehow transforms it from dreadful to doable. So if you feel the need, make a list of where and what the junk harbors are before you start, and then sort and separate your attack into some kind of order. Even if you don't follow that exact order, this exercise will trim back the intimidation and give you a sense of purpose and an overall agenda.

Here is one determined dejunker's plan:

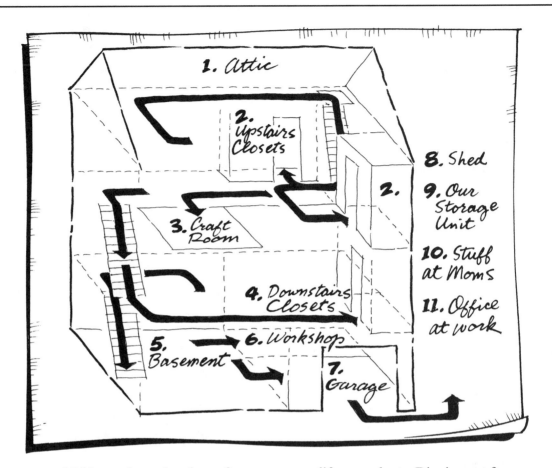

1. Attic
2. Upstairs Closets
3. Craft Room
4. Downstairs Closets
5. Basement
6. Workshop
7. Garage
8. Shed
9. Our Storage Unit
10. Stuff at Moms
11. Office at work
2.

Making a plan only takes a few minutes but it gives you the big picture and a good choice of places to start. And once even a little area is conquered it lends momentum to the others.

Choose your attack pattern

Once you have your plan, how should you put it in action now? Decide which of the following basic strategies best fits your caches and your circumstances.

• **All in one shot**—A wonderful idea, but unfortunately not quite possible for most of us who really

qualify as packrats. Digging out from under years and decades of saving could take as much as several months of nonstop effort, and most of us just don't have that much time off from work. But should you happen to have the summer off, a long vacation or a sabbatical coming to you, or be between jobs and willing to stay that way for a while, go for it! There's no more life-changing "leave of absence" you could take than this. You'll come out the other end a resurrected being, willing and able to move on to the things that really matter to you at last.

• **All your spare time till it's**

done. Every weekend (or whatever days you have off), every evening, etc., until you're all the way through. Demanding, but it does keep up the momentum.

• **A big kickoff, then steady work from there.** (Love this one!) Take whatever big hunk of time you can get your hands on now and use it to start off with a major attack on your clutter. When you've used up that two weeks or four-day weekend, then tally up the junk-purging still to be done and finish it up, in installments, in your off time from there. The pleasure and sense of progress you'll get from that first big bite will give you the courage to go on.

If any other good-size stretches of time fall your way during this period, use them, of course, to further speed the effort.

• **Just keep chipping away at it.** There are different ways you can do this. You can designate an amount of time you are going to devote to decluttering every day, regardless of everything else you're involved in, and spend just that amount every day (or six days a week, if you prefer). No matter how huge your holdings, this WILL eventually do the job if you just keep at it faithfully. One advantage of this approach is that just thirty minutes or an hour a day is easy to take—you won't get bored, tired, or disgusted. And boy do the results add up fast!

Most folks who use this plan prefer to stick with a single project or area till it's done, then move on to the next. You could also add one dejunking project to every week's cleaning.

It's amazing. After a while, you may discover that you're as hooked on dejunking as you were on collecting and stashing.

No matter which method you use:

Be flexible, because mood is one of your most important allies in dejunking. If you're walking by the woodshed and the sight of all those old cardboard boxes piled out there finally stirs you to action, forget the sewing room sift-through you had on today's agenda and go for the shed. If you're suddenly sick and tired of having no workspace on the kitchen counter, stop right now and MAKE some. When it comes to clutter, mood can move mountains (and in half the time).

Most clutter was attained on the spur of the moment. Maybe that's the right timetable to toss it!

Keep your master list or chart of dejunking targets and objectives posted and up to date and review it regularly. This will give you a sense of direction and control and a way of "keeping score"—you know where you're going and what you intend to do, so even if there are unexpected delays or complications you won't get discouraged.

And just wait until you start that exciting business of marking things off because they're DONE!

Ready a place to place things (critical!)

When you finally get into the frame of mind, be it desperation or duty, to trim down your too much, be sure, before you start, to have an easy to reach and use set of "sacks" or other containers to put things in. Nothing will delay or waylay your progress and break your rhythm and objectivity like having to go through things, pick over them, or pick them, up again after you've winnowed them out once. Don't dump things on the floor or pile them to "pick them up later." A second handling might give something a second wind or a second chance. You want to be able to toss things right into a ready-to-go container. Here are some possibilities:

1. Garbage can
2. "Give it to the kids" box
3. Charity box (Goodwill or the like)
4. "Things worth putting in storage" box
5. Burn or shred it box

LET'S GET STARTED NOW:

Ready…
(The junk is ready to go)
Set…
(You are charted)
GO!
(Get going, and it will go!)

As noted earlier, starting is often the hardest part of decluttering. The jump from thinking about clutter to trashing it is like the first step in anything, often strange, unsure, even awkward. But in minutes you'll be in stride, even booting things out.

Here are a few ideas for getting started.

• **Anyplace that will give a quick payoff.** Somewhere (such as the shed out back or a damp, leaky cellar) where the junk is so awful, so old, so deteriorated and impersonal that you can clear away jumbo garbage cans of it in no time, without a panic, pang, or backward glance. The older a stash, the more quickly it can usually be cleared—our illusions about most of that stuff have aged, too.

• **Anyplace that's easy.** This usually means things to which you have no emotional attachment, such as that stash of corroded cleaning supplies under the kitchen sink. Or that stuff someone else left behind, which it's high time to pack up and send back to them.

• **That sore spot.** That place that got you into all this, the one that bugs and disgusts and impedes you so much you can't tolerate it another minute. The middle drawer of your desk, where you couldn't find a paper clip or a notepad in a hurry if your life depended on it, or your clothes closet, where you just spent an hour looking for your blue suit. Or that thing that just gave you a sore shin or black eye—NEVER AGAIN!

Stuff you're tired of taking flak for might also be a good choice here, or anything that makes an all-too-public mess.

• **Private and personal things.** I'm referring here to totally private and personal little stashes—clutter in boxes, containers, drawers, and trays, wallets and purses and briefcases. Tackle boxes, toolboxes, old gifts, souvenirs, clippings, notes, watches, grooming garbage you've grown out of—all that obsolete personal paraphernalia you've been fumbling through for years to get to the good stuff.

This cleaning of your personal clutter will be **easy, fast,** and rewarding. And once you start using all the new extra room this gives you, you'll be really turned on to tackle the tonnage now. This is great bait for coaxing you into the wonderful world of decluttering. In fact, lay this book down and get up and get going on some of this now!

• **It often helps to start with little places**, to build up your courage for the big. If we start looking at our stuff as truckloads (which in some cases it is) we'll be pretty overwhelmed, reluctant to begin, no matter how clear this weekend might be. If you size it up as "loads" instead (sections instead of cellarfulls), you won't even

flinch before starting. Every home has lots of little places to dejunk, such as the sock or the silverware drawer, the spice rack or the tie rack, the medicine chest or the cedar chest.

The more decluttering you do, the faster and better you'll get at it, the more confidence you'll gain, and the more anti-clutter corpuscles you'll build up in your bloodstream. You'll begin to actually look forward to taking on your next project, to exercising your ever more refined skills on the next target area. You'll know you can do it, and how good you'll feel afterward.

Make yourself a "don't need" list: If you want a real revelation and learning experience next weekend, and a good nudge to get started: sit down or better still, walk around and make a list of the things you have that you really don't need or use now. Little things and big things too (like houses, cars, boats, trailers, and campers).

Your surgeon's kit for shearing through clutter

You probably won't need all of this, but here's a checklist of gear to consider. Tailor your own kit to the kind of junkscape you have to work your way through.

Knife and scissors—for cutting things open and miniaturizing, see p. 118. I like to have dejunking tools so I can snip, rip, and strip "the tiny from the total."

Sturdy stepstool or stepladder—for reaching the upper shelves and top boxes, and forget about the idea of standing on any of that old junk out there instead!

Hand truck—if you have a lot of furniture and heavyweight stuff to move.

Work gloves—If you'll be handling a lot of heavy-duty or exterior stuff, a pair of leather or other sturdy work gloves will be well worth having.

Permanent marker, labels, packing tape, and some of those better boxes from your box stash—for repackaging good stuff, or discards to be sent somewhere.

Your biggest garbage cans and some good strong garbage bags. For sharp or heavy trash a garbage box is better than a bag.

Lambswool duster, canister or wet/dry vac, dustcloth, broom, and spray bottles of all-purpose, disinfectant, and glass cleaner—for the cleanup that always has to be done as you're clearing out.

Dust mask—If you'll be working in ultra-dusty or dirty places, a dust mask might be a good idea, especially if you're allergy prone.

Paper and pencil—for all those great ideas that always come to you when you're dejunking.

Should you get someone to help (will it speed or slow things up?)

Some people like company when they're working (I don't). To me, the biggest value in getting help here is that they will snap up and carry off most of what you dejunk! One person can decide—two will debate. One is quiet progress, with more than one you'll spend most of the time explaining, or weeping together.

If you are the type that works better with a "buddy," bear in mind that not just anyone will do. To aid with the delicate business of decluttering you ideally want a helper with the following qualifications:

- Someone who knows you well enough to understand both your idiosyncrasies and enthusiasms and the realities of your present situation. There is no such thing as general advice about junk, only advice suited to a particular person. What you want here is someone sympathetic, yet practical.
- Someone whose judgment in general you respect. A winner in life.
- Someone who is less "clingy" when it comes to things, than you.
- Someone you won't be embarrassed to bare your most cluttered closet or attic to.
- Someone who is capable of sticking to a project, and not

getting distracted (or for that matter, distracting you).

- Someone who can keep their mouth shut!

Exactly WHAT can this other person or persons do to help you now?

- Fetch and carry, bring things you need.
- Return things or dispose of them.
- Take care of cleanup detail.
- Take care of the kids while you dejunk.
- Lend encouragement and moral support.
- Serve as "dumpster's advocate" whenever necessary.
- Help when you need a "tiebreaker" in the judging process, or even just serve as a sounding board for your own thinking process.

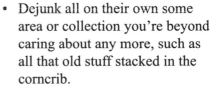

- Dejunk all on their own some area or collection you're beyond caring about any more, such as all that old stuff stacked in the corncrib.
- Your helpers can also help celebrate when you're done!

A good friend of mine, Dave, was helping a friend move and as all of us who have friends with packrat proclivities know, this was no one-trip job. After they'd loaded the friend's farm truck up and sent him off to his new home with a load of stuff, there was no one there but Dave and his truck, which had a sixteen-foot bed and side boards. Dave loaded the thing completely full with junk, like flat bike tires, crushed baskets, stacks of ten-year-old newspapers, broken lamps, and old faucet parts. He quickly took the entire load to the junkyard instead of the new home and dumped it. Then he hustled back and was loading the better stuff when the friend returned. The friend never missed one single item and to this day doesn't have a clue that half a semi load of his "too much" is gone.

Many of you reading this (who are quickly recounting recent moves and wondering if a "Dave" helped or not) could do the same service for yourself, much to your benefit. And there will be no regrets or misgivings because **you** will be the picker and sorter.

Basics of the unburying process

When you're faced with wall-to-wall, floor-to-ceiling clutter such as in a junk room, storage bin, or attic, the first thing you want to do is make yourself some room to work. So start with the biggest things and the things within reach right now that are the easiest to eliminate.

Once you have a clearing, it helps to have an empty table in it for your smaller tools and supplies, and to use for sorting. If you can't find a table in the stash, a card table or folding table will do fine.

You will also need some room for sorting, and for those piles or boxes of stuff you collect as you sort, such as Baby Things to Give Away, or Books for the Used Book Store. It's always more efficient to collect a bunch or boxful of whatever before you start packaging it up or carrying it off to its new home.

After you have room to maneuver, you can either tackle the stacks systematically from one end to the other, or pick off the next pile that appeals to you, wherever it may be. Since the will to weed through something is more than half the battle, **go with impulse** whenever you can.

A collection of small things such as a drawer full of odds and ends or a box of ancient who-knows-what is often best emptied onto your tabletop, or a dropcloth or old sheet on the floor. There's something about seeing it all spread out that clears the judgment cells in the brain, plus you have to pick it up to put it back in the box, so you'll be more prone to dump it!

Once you get started, don't let yourself be interrupted or sidetracked. If you come across the long-lost pocketknife or watch in your excavations, or a truly amazing photo of yourself as a trim young thing, don't stop now to "wow." Set that little treasure in the Treasure Box underneath your table, and keep on going. The same goes for sudden impulses to try and find the other candlestick now that you've unearthed this one, or to sprint out to the shed and see if the rain fly to this lovely tent might still be around somewhere. Don't run to the phone and start making calls to see if you can still get parts for that old pressure cooker, either. If your friend Susie stops by to catch up on things, make a date for some other time or ask her if she minds keeping you company while you keep at it. Or talk her into taking away some stuff—use interruptions positively. Stick with dejunking, till you've finished your target area or your quota of trashing time for the day.

If you are not the only inhabitant of your house, and you're working somewhere in the public domain, such as a linen closet in a hallway, beware of gutting the whole thing at once unless you've got the entire day to work on it. We packrats can really pack it in and you will simply not believe how much will come out of there. It'll be frustrating to everyone if your time runs out while there are still piles and heaps out and around everywhere. Better to proceed a shelf or layer at a time in such situations, and to stick with one such project before starting a new one.

Dejunking doesn't necessarily mean trash it all. Almost everything benefits from condensing. Condensing is dejunking too—there often is some good in amidst all that chaff. Mail or old papers, for example, are usually about three quarters obsolete stuff and packaging and one quarter pure ore.

Persist with your list

As you work your way through your "too much," you may start muttering to yourself and wondering why you kept this and that (and for so long). You might get a little disgusted or discouraged now as you realize what is at hand and ahead. You're often working in hot, cramped, and dusty places, and don't have much support from others. You've done a lot, but there seems to be so much more to do. And worst of all is the emotional drain it can be, going through all that old stuff, especially paper clutter or sentimental savings. But in any kind of clutter, really, there

is all kinds of evidence of unachieved ambitions, past illusions, forgotten plans, failed good intentions, neglect, carelessness, even unkindness on our part. Three or four hours of plowing through things like this can leave us more exhausted than a day of ditch digging. So don't be surprised and don't be derailed by this. Expect it and remember you are burying this clutter in the ditch forever, carry on with your carrying out.

It may also help to:

• **Vary your dejunking diet**. If you've done six hours of paper and you can't take any more, spend the last two hours on garden or garage junk. Alternating the types of projects you take on: indoor/outdoor, mostly mental/mostly physical, will help

keep dejunker's dejection to a minimum. Or go pulverize something with a sledge hammer!

• **Stop now and start again tomorrow**. We almost always feel better the next morning about things. This is also a good reason to schedule the toughest dejunking assignments for early in the day, when you're still feeling fresh and optimistic. It's easy to say "Well, I'll do an hour of that each night after I get home from work," and a lot harder to actually do.

• **There is nothing wrong with dejunking on the Sabbath**. In fact, I can't think of a more spiritual thing to do.

• **Remind yourself of the rewards** of how nice it will be to have an uncramped clothes closet at last, or how much more you'll enjoy this space when it's your new exercise room or study rather than a junk room.

• Some folks keep themselves going by **forcing the issue**. They start dejunking the yard now and invite everyone they know to a big lawn party at the end of the month, or the end of the summer.

• (I've saved the best for last here.) **Check out one of my other books on dejunking**, especially *Clutter's Last Stand*, to strengthen your sense of WHY you're doing all this. An hour or two of perusing these pages will get you going again, I guarantee it, and it'll be fun, too. My book *Clutter Free! Finally & Forever* has lots of "before and after" confessions which you'll find inspiring and helpful.

Is it Treasure or Tonnage?
(How to sift, sort, and select)

"Junk judging" is the very heart of decluttering—deciding what to keep and what should go. That "ALL" that you have, you probably had a good reason (at the time) to get it, each and every piece of it. And you might think you need to **keep** each and every bit of it.

But there is an important principle here regarding the stifling effect of too much that Mother Nature has tried to teach us for centuries. It applies to all living things, and the principle is called "thinning."

At first it seems to go against all good sense and decency, the idea of getting rid of perfectly good "whatevers." My first lesson in this came in the sugar beet fields of the record-crop-per-acre Magic Valley in Idaho. The beets would be planted in spring, and before long the seedlings literally sprang out of the fertile ground. Before long we went into the fields and hacked and cut and hoed about three quarters of those beautiful, healthy little plants down. Brutal it was, indeed, to leave only one plant every eight or ten inches, where before there were five or six. We did this with the carrots and the corn, too, seemingly a temporary insanity of destroying what was flourishing. But time proved it a wise and profitable move, as with the room to grow, those little seedlings grew into large, beautiful, plants, yielding a-plenty. Any that didn't happen to be thinned, left in initially healthy clumps, soon crowded each other and a dwarfed, scrawny, clump of nothing was the result. And here is the kicker: **if you waited too long to thin**, it was too late. The plants were too massed and jammed together to be separated without harm. They were out of control and you could only sit back and watch the waste.

Likewise, people or places that are crowded by clutter in time become limited, distorted, and twisted. Here, too, thinning and pruning aids blooming, And when it comes to our stuff, **now is the time**.

Junk judging guidelines

How can you **decide**, in the presence of that pile of "too much," what is junk and what isn't?

First—your clutter is your call

I receive requests constantly to make professional visits or house

You know... stashing all your junk in that thing doesn't make it Treasure.

calls to deal with people's clutter for them. I've refused all such offers, at any price. There is just no way I can judge the weight or worth of your treasures. Value has a great deal to do with inner emotion, and never can we know someone else's soul well enough to make a just judgment call on their things.

YOU have to decide, your stuff is your business, not mine, your spouse or family's, or a consultant's. Only you know your mind and heart, your dreams and values, and the point you've reached now. Only you know the history of your things and the strength of your ties to them. Do they fit you now, or not? YOU judge junk!

A teddy bear with both ears missing, serious stains, and leaking stuffing isn't junk if the kids use it and love it. A new Lexus car (that you don't drive often or really need) in your garage could be total junk. The TIME you've had something, or how much it COST isn't really a factor in the disposal decision, either. Who had it before or where you got it isn't really important either.

I suggest a little "judging" guideline sheet. (Honest answers, now!)

JUNK JUDGING GUIDELINES

VALUE FACTOR	QUESTION
Life enhancement	Is it enhancing the quality of your life **NOW**? ☐ Yes ☐ No
Use/activity	It's there—do you really use it? ☐ Yes ☐ No
Fit	Does it, will it, fit anymore? (Or have you outgrown it?) ☐ Yes ☐ No
Place	Do you really have a place or space (on, in, or around you) for it? ☐ Yes ☐ No
Does it love YOU?	Does owning it bless, inspire, and expand you— love you back? ☐ Yes ☐ No

You call it...
and NOW is better than later!

When sorting and deciding what goes and what stays, remember that how long you've had something, how much it cost, who gave it to you, when, and why, whether it was handmade or imported and all of that, is not the determining factor for retainment. Just quit loving things that have stopped loving you back. Fortunately, we outgrow many things, and need to face the present and future without lugging along the past. So ask yourself the ultimate question with each article:

"Does this now, or will it in the future, enhance my life (or others' lives)."

If the answer is no, a good, solid, clear-cut **no**, then get it out of your life any way you can. There is no room for "moderation" here—if something is worthless to you, there's no need to keep it around you!!

> "An important word here is passion. If you are passionate about something, it is important to you and therefore not junk. If a thing or activity does not create passion or excitement or they have waned, then it's time to dejunk."

Yes, you CAN get rid of things
you are tired of!

"When our six-year-old to-be-adopted-daughter arrived by airplane from Texas, she had with her one suitcase of clothes, one suitcase of books, and **three bushels of stuffed toys**! Several months later I got after her about cleaning up her room, and she sat down on the floor, burst into tears, and screamed, 'I have too much stuff!'

'Then get rid of some of it,' I said.

She looked up, her face suddenly radiant, and said, 'You mean I **can**?'

Two days later, we took two bushels of stuffed toys to the charity collection center. From the remaining bushel, she stored a few at her oldest sister's apartment for overnight stays, gave several away to neighbor children, and kept a modest few for herself. Now, at sixteen, she has exactly one teddy bear left from those three bushels. Meanwhile her twin cousins, with whom she lived until she came to us, have filled a ten-foot-long built-in bookcase entirely with stuffed animals. And Alicia, every three or four months, carefully sorts her possessions and loads things she no longer uses into plastic bags for us to take to the thrift store. **Her** built-in bookcase has one shelf of her favorite books, one shelf of photographs she likes to display, and one shelf strewn with flowers she dried herself with a few treasures such as a collection of seashells artistically arranged among them.

But I don't think I will ever forget her awed delight at realizing she was actually allowed to get rid of things she was tired of. Sometimes she goes overboard—she has given away three beds, two dressers, a computer and printer, and a few chairs, but she will never be a slave to her possessions."

If in doubt throw it out?

I really don't like the old adage, "If in doubt, throw it out." A lot of mistakes are made that way. I would counsel you to not be in doubt. If in doubt, find out. And **then** decide whether to keep it or throw it out.

I also disagree with the old saw, "If you haven't used it in six months (or a year), get rid of it." I haven't used my Scout uniform for four years, but I'm not going to get rid of it, haven't used my shotgun for twelve years, and I'm not going to get rid of it, haven't used my sleds for three years (not enough snow in Idaho the last three winters), but I'm not going to get rid of them. And I haven't used my fire extinguisher for fifteen years, and I'm surely not going to toss it out.

The length of time you've owned something is immaterial—two minutes could be too long and twenty years not long enough to own some-thing. Asking yourself "does this enhance my life?" or "Will it?" is the key—use or honest potential use.

Remember: the past is to learn from, not live in

We are slow to let go of what we used to be and that is good in a way. But the past is to learn from, not live in, and getting rid of what we used to be is for the most part a real plus. The old and the used to be are ballast that holds us back from our voyage to where we want to be, more than we ever imagine. If much of what you used to be wasn't really a blessing, it wasn't what you had in mind or you never felt good about it, then dump it for sure. Get it out of the album, out of the records, out of the clothes closet, out of the attic—and leave some room for what you **want** to be.

Don't backslide!

Backsliding, believe it or not (sneaking back to the garbage bag or dumpster to recover something you've already ditched) can be a real problem for a packrat.

What we need, folks, is a computer "mouse" attached to our stuff, so we can move that little arrow to an item, then move the item over to a little garbage can icon, hit the button, and the thing is trashed, gone forever, unrecoverable. I've watched people edit manuscripts, remove all the junk and trash from them this way. And if I were an inventor this is what I would come up with, for the greatest of all clutter cures.

You need to dump something the day you determine it is detrimental to your daily living. Don't let it lay in "wake" in the parlor to be pawed over by anyone who might think they need to review it in case temporary insanity caused you to send it to the happy hunting grounds. Resurrected clutter is a ghost you don't need around to haunt you any longer.

The very name "odds and ends" ought to give us a clue when it comes to making a judgment on value.

What about those antiques?

You might get the impression, from reading my now five books on decluttering, that I am a heartless destroyer of valuable keepsakes. It's just the opposite—I have a soft spot for keepsakes and antiques, and an avid appreciation of them. I have a now world-famous cleaning museum, and I'm constantly on the lookout for new (old!) pieces for it.

Antiques are well worth oohing and ahhing over—they carry feelings, reminders, and lessons from the past that we all need for inner nourishment and a better future life. But too many fine antiques are either accidentally destroyed or buried in clutter, and thus are never available to be seen or used. Antiques lost in attics or piles are worthless to both the owner and the public. For many years now my mission has been to find such things, protect them, and make them productive. Why let them rust and ruin until they merit tossing?

Old doesn't always mean "gold"

One problem here is the tendency to think everything old is valuable, and that is far from the truth. We've heard stories or watched a TV show where an old antique lamp or etching turns out to be worth $265,000! Maybe so… but those are rare one-in-a-million chances, folks, so don't let something you don't like or really even have room for hold onto you forever because you hold out hopes that it might be a treasure. We've all heard talk of such successes springing out of sacks in the attic, but in more than fifty years in the profession of helping people to clean up and look after their possessions, and at least two decades of researching and writing about saved stuff, I have yet to meet or see in person, one single, bona-fide trash to treasure story.

On a major media (radio and TV) tour I was on once, we asked callers and audiences to let us in on any incident or case where a great fortune was made from one of their pieces of old saved stuff. Guess what! In all of those broadcasts we received not one single response! That big "might" we often have in back of our mind somewhere when it comes to old stuff often turns out to be a "mite."

So let's be more realistic about the stuff we keep, and weigh the cost of keeping with the true chance of its someday value to an outside market. Remember, 250 million others in this country alone have garages, attics, basements, and storage sheds full of the same or similar stuff.

We all think our old stuff is going to be valuable some-day, simply because "it's old." But a goodly percent of old stuff is worthless.

Make this weekend the moment of truth!

If in doubt, find out now, instead of pushing the item in question to the back for later. If you run into something you feel has historic or personal value, deal with it this weekend, not later! Consult an expert, and have it examined and appraised.

One great discovery I've made visiting antique shops looking for old cleaning pieces for my museum is how competent the owners of such shops are, even in the smallest towns. These people have clubs and connections and an impressive expertise. They know where and how to get information for you if they don't have it. And best of all I really trust these people. If you have a rare something worth $2500, they won't tell you $25 or $250, and try to buy it. Their eyes will light up and they will be enthusiastic for you!

So walk in and ask or show—don't delay. Waiting has caused more waste of good stuff than all the floods and fires of the centuries.

If it is an antique then act on it—take care of it, put it to work for me and others to see and benefit from. If you need money, sell it.

Antique agenda
Check it out *(NOW)—If you really believe an item may have value, get it appraised to confirm that it is worth keeping.*

Show and share it*! If it's good, let family and fellow man get the benefit of it. Clean it up, repair or restore it, and put it on display somewhere.*

Or Sell it*! and spend or invest the money in some better way for you.*

There is a great magazine, called *America's Most Wanted*, PO Box 17107, Little Rock AR 72212. It will give you an instant education in how many collectors there are out there and what they are looking for. When it comes to antiques there are experts in everything from brass blowtorches to Dixie cup lids, corkscrews to ship logbooks and diaries, old telephones to Boy Scout stuff, boxing to big band memorabilia, Japanese swords to sidesaddles, Civil War collectibles to cigar labels, oyster-related objects to old poison bottles. This magazine details hundreds of such enthusiasms, probably covering every piece of "possible antique" stuff you have. So if in doubt, get a copy and page through it. It will be the most fascinating reading you've done recently, the start of a great step to freedom, and who knows, maybe even some hard cash.

No-mess access

What we decide to do with the stuff we don't do away with, is as important as the decision to keep it. If it ends up unaccessible again, we might just as well have ditched it. This is a good thing to keep in mind when making decisions. Keepers aren't keepers if you have no place to keep them for easy access. It's your call, but figure it out or *throw it out*!

Once you have your worthwhile things stored so that you can get to them easily, you want to go through them often.

Let me give an example from my own life. As my books sold ever more copies and I became better known, I was fortunate to be put in touch with many outstanding people. These were mostly women, because women usually were the experts in cleaning and home management, the subjects I concentrated. At home, in the media and as I travelled around the country and the world, I also couldn't help noticing that women usually ran things better than men. I met so many sharp, insightful, incredibly helpful women that I started a drawer called "The World's 100 Most Wanted Women" (anticipating perhaps hiring some of them or using them as consultants or research sources). I kept on adding to it over time and it finally got so full that there wasn't one single person I was recontacting, following up on, or sending copies of my new books to, as I'd planned, because it wasn't a list of people—it was a mass of "stuff." When something that would have been of interest to one of them did come up, or a time or place cropped up for meeting with one of them, I couldn't get to what I needed easily enough to benefit either of us.

Then I learned an important rule of storage: don't just go through stored things, but go through them **often**. Our purpose, our intentions, and our reasons change daily, weekly, yearly, even hourly, and some times and opportunities pass. Often both the rhyme and the reason for which you originally kept something have totally faded and the matter is closed, so why keep it around and in the way of things?

Waiting years to go through things is too long. Going through your saved stuff every few months and freshening it up is pure pleasure. In a single hour one day I reduced the "100 most wanted" drawer by two thirds, and renewed some of the most beneficial contacts. The value in keeping anything is in keeping it current and

accessible… instantly! Anything else stored is questionable.

Beware of "junk bunkers"

In your efforts to evict the excess in your life, beware the two-edged sword called "organizers"—shelves, baskets, binders, boxes, racks, pigeonhole devices, containers of all kinds, even furnishings like china and curio cabinets. There are no end of

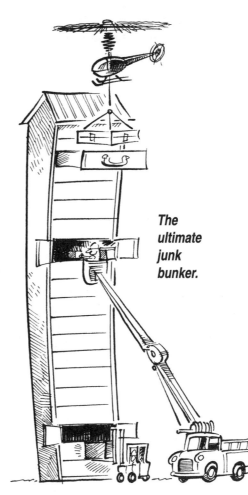

The ultimate junk bunker.

miracle devices today that once bought, will "instantly put everything you have in order." Don't you believe it. First of all, **you** have to do the organizing, and second, organizers often just give us the excuse and means to keep and store more. Remember the first principle of packrattery: Stuff will accumulate proportionate to the space and place made available for it.

Moving around, or organizing things we ought to get rid of ends up just being a long-term game of musical chests (or drawers).

Clever organizers (like a trash compactor in the home or office) can take a mass of clutter and condense it to a smaller size. The fact that it now takes up less space is so admirable that we forget it is still there—just as heavy, and just as useless. What needs to removed from our place ought to be evicted now, not squeezed into a smaller, more convenient size to be carried around till later. Renaming things, or creating some elaborate filing system or category for them, doesn't change what they are. Clutter is still clutter even if it is computer-ized, or housed in neat plastic containers.

Promises like "unique storage solutions" usually translate to: "we can stack it—clutter and all—higher, tighter, and neater." And for what closet organizing companies and the like can't fit in the closet, they will provide accessories for, to screw onto doors and walls and accommodate the rest. No matter how creatively arranged or superbly stacked, **clutter is still clutter**.

Flinch first when you see an organizer, then visualize what will end up in it, and you'll probably pass it by, and be glad you did.

"My biggest mistake in dejunking was trying to organize what I needed to get rid of." Don't get carried away with organizing stuff… carry as much of it as you can away first! You don't have to organize it, if you don't have it!

Most of us don't get rid of clutter, we just get a bigger box (or a bigger house, the biggest junk bunker of all!)

Now...
what should you do with what you weeded out?

**ONE GOOD PLACE
TO DISPOSE OF IT IS:
*AMERICA'S FIRST ANSWER,
FRONTLINE ATTACK ON "TOO
MUCH"***

...the Garage Sale!

Garage sales—holding one is a good idea, because it gets things back into circulation, which is one solution for "too much." A garage sale also causes enough work, frustration,

embarrassment, and reflection to inspire us, next time, to buy and keep less. God bless garage sales (as long as my wife doesn't go!)!

A few good garage sale guidelines (to really move that merchandise out)

CLEAN IT—Use disinfectant cleaner and inform people "I've cleaned this with Slapacide." People fear other people's germs.

PRICE IT—Not what you over-paid, or the "recovery" or "revenge" price, but more along the lines of: "Someone will haul this off for me

and it will have a good home."

DISPLAY IT—Anything up off the ground or sidewalk sells better, so make or rent tables and cover them.

POOL IT—Combo presentations (yours and your neighbors' goods) draw more of each other's relatives, and will double or triple sales.

TRY THE HONOR SYSTEM— Place a self-serve cash box where people can toss in money and take change, most people are honest. (Just keep $20 or $50 in it.) People buy more if they don't have to face a clerk to buy a used bra or a motorless lawn mower.

Now vow "this will be my last"—and make it so!

Another good way to dispose of your "weedouts"

From a relieved packrat in Madison, Wisconsin:

"One thing that has helped me to get rid of stuff to which I feel especially attached emotionally is to give it to individuals rather than institutions. I had a large number of books about the Middle Ages, for example, many of them beautifully illustrated. I knew I'd never read them again, but somehow I couldn't bear to part with them. Until I met a young man (the son of my investment broker) who was majoring in German Medieval history in college. His delight and gratitude in receiving the books somehow filled the emotional hole created by my giving them up. Similarly, I recently (albeit reluctantly) packed up loads of quality clothes in excellent condition that are no longer appropriate to my present lifestyle. Instead of donating them to a Goodwill store, I brought them to a local shelter for men recovering from addictions. Seeing some of the men face to face who would be wearing my clothes gave me a feeling of warmth that more than compensated for any sense of loss over the clothing I was surrendering."

Don't let creeping doubts override the impulse to be generous. Later "maybe" values are mighty remote— you aren't throwing the baby out with the bath water, just the water now, the tub later, and the baby never!

CHAPTER 5

Clutter at a Glance

This chapter is a short course in the most common and troublesome kinds of clutter inhabiting the modern home and office—where they live, what they look like, what harm they do us, and how to make short work of them!

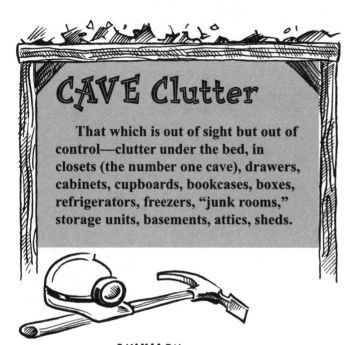

CAVE Clutter

That which is out of sight but out of control—clutter under the bed, in closets (the number one cave), drawers, cabinets, cupboards, bookcases, boxes, refrigerators, freezers, "junk rooms," storage units, basements, attics, sheds.

SUMMARY:

In caves like this is where our lives' leftovers languish. Much of this stuff is where it is because (except for winter clothes and Christmas decorations) it doesn't get much use. It is lying in wake, awaiting a burial of some kind, although most of it has been temporarily buried by other clutter. You might say it's in the coffin, but not yet in the ground!.

The amount of cave clutter we have usually parallels our decision-stalling ability, and because all this stuff is hidden we think it doesn't hurt. Cave clutter loves to laugh at us as we move it in from somewhere else, cram it in, shuffle it from shelf to shelf, pore over it, hunt through it, fold and refold it, arrange and rear-range it, forever trying to fit more in, and dreaming up excuses for it. Often as much as fifty percent of cave clutter is unneeded, and if we were honest about it, unwanted.

SOLUTION:

To clean out a cave you have to go in, not just keep passing by. That means all the way in, or what is in back of, under, and behind will remain forever. Up to now we have just removed the overflow or in the way stuff, dodging anything that is difficult to get through or around. Pull it all out, and you'll know what to eliminate. As for the good stuff, condense it, re-box it (don't leave it rattling around loose), and mark the box on all four sides and the top with a marker. This will jog your memory or help others the next time around. Otherwise, you or others will be forced to open and go through every box, when you're getting ready to move, desperate to find something, or faced with a fire or flood situation. Or when someone else (after your departure from this planet) has to deal with it all.

When you're finished, you've eliminated the fire, odor, or safety hazard, regained the use of some of your most convenient storage space, and have room for fresh and impor-tant future stuff.

For more on Cave Clutter see Chapter 6 of *Clutter's Last Stand*, Chapters 6 and 8 of *Not for Packrats Only*, and Chapter 6 of *Clutter Free!*

SUMMARY:

The accessible "tops" in our living space were meant for purposes other than storing and stacking. When they are covered with clutter it causes confusion, breakage, and lack of privacy, and impedes use and cleaning of the item this happens to be the top of. When you consider those cluttered tops of dressers, chests of drawers, counters, tables, refrigerators, work benches, night tables, end tables, desks, window ledges, bookcases, and credenzas, it all adds up to a top traffic jam.

SOLUTION:

Putting things on a top overnight, or while you're actually using the area is great—you have a place to put something and you put it there. The sin here is not in using the top, but leaving the mess behind when you're done. When you clear your project out, clear it ALL out. It only takes seconds to transfer things to a drawer, cupboard, box, or compartment right under, over, or beside the top area, so you can keep a clean, clear top. Hanging tools and other things right over the use area is even handier than heaping them on top!

GOAL:

Tops that are easy to clean and can be USED for whatever they need to be used for. Uncluttered tops that reduce anxieties and improve aesthetics (look good!)

ON TOP OF Stuff

Keys, change, pills, coins, clothing, gloves, wallets, cufflinks, jewelry, books, watches, pens, cards, instructions to things, junk mail, bills, catalogs, newspapers, magazines, hankies, cosmetics, drugs, grooming aids, tools, finished or unfinished projects, things on their way somewhere.

For more on trimming down "top of" clutter, see Chapter 8 of *Not for Packrats Only*, and Chapters 9 and 10 of *The Office Clutter Cure*.

One woman sent me a long list of everything unneeded she found on her dressertops, from broken flutes to Harley Davidson patches, old eyeglasses to miniature chess sets to used Q-tips. Her final deduction was, "It is truly amazing what can fit on the 12" x 36" top of a dresser."

CLOTHES

Suits, dresses, blouses, shirts, skirts, slacks, sweaters, jackets, robes, coats, formals, athletic wear, sweatshirts, T-shirts, uniforms, vests, coveralls, shorts, swimsuits, long johns, novelty clothes, shoes, socks, scarves, gloves, ties, belts, hats, caps.

SUMMARY:

Wardrobes are often one of our worst cases of "too much." We must be reminded, it seems, that we have only one head, two hands, two feet, and a torso. You can waste a lot of life pawing through closets and drawers full of clothes, worrying about fashion, matching, moths, and storage of rarely or never used apparel. Just because you paid for it once, doesn't mean you have to keep on paying. If you had just one of each of the clothes listed above you would have thirty pieces to wear, wash, and worry about. If you have two of each that means sixty and three of each, ninety. Need I go on? Too much! Overwhelming! And for what?

SOLUTION:

The judgments here will be easy if you remember that the bottom line on clothes is wearing, not wishing. Clothing clutter is mostly vanity motivated, so your clothes quotient right now should tell you something about your personality.

Should you keep them?
Six smart ways to clear the closet:

- Outfits that don't fit are OUT!
- Anything uncomfortable should go!
- Retire what looks better on the hanger than on you.
- Too nice to stain may be too nice to remain.
- Panic or impulse-purchased clothes are almost always pass-on-able.
- Herds of rarely-worn hats and shoes require year-round roundup.

The old "second hand" solution is still the best. Pass your culls on to others—the needy, greedy, or seedy.

GOAL:

An uncrowded closet that gives you easy, wrinkle-free selection, and cuts out all that rummaging, try-on, and fretting time.

For more on coping with clothes clutter, see Chapter 9 of *Clutter's Last Stand*, Chapter 8 of *Not for Packrats Only*, and Chapter 6 of *Clutter Free! Finally and Forever*.

SUMMARY:

Most of us have 25% more furniture than we need or are currently using, and sad to say, we are always looking and shopping for more to replace some that really doesn't need replacing. Most furniture doesn't wear out (some actually lasts centuries, not just lifetimes). Furniture can ugly out from poor care, lack of repair, or we just get tired of it. But we have a hard time letting furniture of any kind "go," so instead we put it in the basement or another room, or store it in the garage, or at grandma's house. We fight unneeded furniture, hoard it, refuse to give it away until the mice, sun, rain, or people running into it finally do it in. Then we can throw it out.

SOLUTION:

1. Be slow, real slow to replace furniture. Once you start thinking about, and looking at, new furniture (most of which you don't really need), there is no stopping and you do real dumb things.

2. Remember how when you first moved away from home or got married, how long and well you got along with "early orangecrate" furnishings?

3. Once you commit to the new, you need to commit for the old at the same time. Don't move one thing in without a clear and committed destination for the piece being replaced. Old furniture motto—out of the room, out of your life.

4. If you need furniture only for a

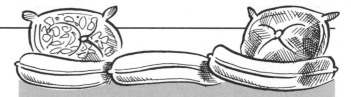

FURNITURE Clutter

Chairs and more chairs, overstuffed, wing-backed, upright, captain's, beanbag and blow up chairs, extra office chairs, recliners, couches, sofas, loveseats, futons, hidabeds, roll-away beds, desks, shelves, beds, dressers, nightstands, armoires, cribs, lamps, coffee tables, dining room tables, end tables, card tables, TV trays, and other tables with leaves and extensions, hutches, knickknack and whatnot and showcase and corner cupboards, baker's racks, buffets, butler carts, ottomans, stools, and cushions.

while, rent it, or use the floor. Nothing is worse than having lots of furniture to move and a too-small house to put it in.

5. Buy the best when you buy the first time and most of your furniture clutter problems will be over. You'll be so poor you can't buy any more and the quality of the pieces you do have will eliminate the need to buy any more.

GOAL:

To have only the furniture you need and have it where it belongs, for a long, long time. Keep it clean and in good repair so that people will treat it as they should.

For more on freeing yourself of unnecessary furniture, see Chapter 6 of _Not for Packrats Only_, pp. 54, 61, and 62 of _The Office Clutter Cure_, and pp. 137-140 of _Clutter Free!_

PHOTOS

Slides, color prints, black and whites, Polaroids, videos, film, used and unused, negatives, portraits, cheap shots, pictures of graduations, sweethearts, weddings, and trips.

SUMMARY:

Photographs have one purpose and value—**to be seen!** Basements across the country house photos of every type, waiting for… what? For the cellar to flood, so we can weep and groan over our lost heritage. Photos today are easy to take, and can easily multiply to too many to keep track of. The valuable ones are lost in the piles, and never seen or appreciated. Why do we keep every single thing that ever comes back from the developer? Those fuzzy pictures aren't going to come into focus, nor the red-eyed ones fade, or those missing heads grow back on.

While we're at it, how many cameras (and accessories) do you have? How many work? Do you use?

THE SOLUTION IS A SIMPLE "S.O.S." (SAVE OUR SLIDES!):

S. Sort

Go through all your photos. Toss the ruined, fourth-rate, and unidentifiable ones. Trim the total number down, organize them by subject or year or whatever, and then mark the ones that really matter. Doing this with another person or persons is a good idea, it will speed the process. Sort the pictures into separate piles: to be copied, enlarged, framed, or whatever. Toss those envelopes, etc., pictures come back in—they only add to the pile. Negatives are small and thin; a lifetime's worth can be stored in a little dark box. Trash obviously worthless ones, put the others into labeled envelopes, and keep them until you die.

O. Offer

Select and send off the photos that don't mean much to you, but will touch or enhance others' lives. Include the negative if you can find it, along with a note, and it might result in getting a valuable picture back from them.

S. Show

Photos always have a place, at home or at work, on walls, in stands, in albums or scrapbooks. Mount the best photos and put them up on the wall, or in some place where they are accessible, organized, and can be used (seen). Or convert them to video.

Once photos are out of boxes and into full view or appreciative ownership, beholders and new owners will weep in your arms for joy at the reminders and memory stimuli. Photos can teach, motivate, inspire, and create interest and valuable relationships.

GOAL:

All the photos you have, and any being taken now or in the future, made instantly accessible and usable. Use photos to actively enhance life, not just record it. Enlarge good shots and send them constantly for gifts.

For more on putting photos in focus, see page 141-45 of *Clutter's Last Stand* and pages 69-70 of *Not for Packrats Only*.

GIFTS

Christmas, birthday, Mother's Day, Father's Day, Grandparent's Day, Secretary's Day, Valentine's Day, Easter, and at least 20 other gift-giving days. Housewarming gifts, friendship gifts, going away, coming home, wedding, retirement, promotion, graduation, anniversary. Plaques, trophies, awards, pins, badges!

SUMMARY:

Sure, they aren't of our own choosing, but we're the ones who keep them—for what, and for how long? "But someone gave it to me" is not a valid excuse for entombing something forever. Black eyes and rattlesnakes can be given, too. Gifts are meant to convey the best of feelings, not to become a burden.

SOLUTION:

Believe and practice "It's the thought that counts."

Remember, a gift is just the transmitter of affection, not the affection itself. When you get a gift, concentrate on the giver ("How thoughtful Maggie is!") rather than on the object they happened to give. Savor the love, care, kindness, cash, and maybe even hard work that went into the gift, and how genuinely the giver intended to please you. And

then deal with it like any other item in your dejunking program—do I like this, do I need it, or not? If you don't ever intend to use it, don't really want to look at it, and refuse to display it, better to move it out.

If there are any regrettables among those receivables:

- Use them, put them in service, wear them out
- Trade or exchange them for something you do want
- Take a photo of them for sentiment and then pass them on
- Give them to any admirer of them
- Leave them lying around in public in a nice box
- Dissect them for usable parts
- Give or will them back to the givers

GOAL:

As much as you can, free yourself of the politics of overdone gift giving and receiving and reciprocating and acknowledging (and then tending). Don't be a junk gift giver yourself. Visit people when they are sick or in need instead. It's the best gift of all, the most remembered, and creates zero clutter. Caring for the sick and lonely can seldom reach "too much."

For more on graceful gift divestment, see Chapter 7 of *Clutter's Last Stand* and Chapter 8 of *Not for Packrats Only.*

SUMMARY:

There were twenty, then two hundred (like *Look, Life, The Saturday Evening Post, Reader's Digest*) not long ago. By the seventies, all subjects were covered by about 1,500 magazines—today there are at least 3,500 different ones, so if you think you might be going to manage to keep up, forget it! Magazines aren't the prime source of information; you won't find much here that takes a solid stand (truth is controversial, and too many advertisers would be offended). So magazines are mostly innocuous, middle-of-the-road stuff. Magazines are getting more and more expensive ($3 a copy or more) and one "hooker" or lead article on the cover in bold letters (like "SEX") is supposed to justify buying the whole thing. Magazines are hard to keep up with (twelve magazines a month is 1200 pages to deal with, forty a day!), and guilt-producing when we don't. They pile up fast, in the living room and the attic.

MAGAZINES

Professional, technical, household, entertainment, in-flight, women's, men's, children's, news magazines, religious magazines, association and organization magazines, magazines about food, gardening, woodworking, automobiles (this list could go on to fill the page…).

SOLUTION:

The majority of most magazines is advertising, which is updated monthly, so keeping them doesn't really make sense. Magazines should be handled once—scan them immediately, as soon as you get them. Remove the few things you want to read later or save, and chuck the rest in the recycle bin. Magazines take zero concentration, so if you keep them handy to deal with during waiting time, commercials, or at those early or late hours of the day, you can pick and peruse the edifying and discard the rest. If you get a backup of five magazines to read, you are beginning to be buried. Cutting down (the number of subscriptions you have) and keeping up is the solution for magazine "too much."

GOAL:

Not getting any magazines you aren't interested enough in to process promptly. Reading this month's before next month's arrives. Saving only articles you really want—never the whole magazine.

For more on magazines, see Chapter 8 of *Clutter's Last Stand* and *Not for Packrats Only*, and Chapter 6 of *Clutter Free! Finally and Forever*.

BOOKS

Texts, cookbooks, novels, how to, reference, idle reading, children's books, schoolbooks, professional books, directories, manuals, record books, tally books, religious books, racy books, gift books, encyclopedias, atlases, secondhand books, antiques, borrowed books, books we never took back to the library.

SUMMARY:

Books fill our shelves and the shelves of bookstores, and new ones are pouring forth from the presses at the rate of more than 50,000 a year. Add in what we have piled and stored, and what we've borrowed, loaned, or lusted after, and we have "too much."

Because books were once rare and precious, we are hesitant to relieve our shelves of them. When I was growing up, defacing or discarding a book was about even with adultery. But today being a book doesn't sanctify anything or guarantee the contents, and the total materials cost in a book these days is probably less than lunch at McDonalds.

Only about 20 percent of the books we keep around are actually used or even looked at occasionally, and a book has value only when and if it is read. Books are HEAVY and they take up a lot of room.

SOLUTION:

Books we could do without usually fall into the following categories:

- ❑ Obsolete/out of date—anything from old phone directories to Factory Outlet Guide 1965
- ❑ Damaged—broken, mouse-chewed, ripped, or waterstained
- ❑ Unfinished—so dull we haven't made it beyond page 30 in three starts
- ❑ Gift books—we didn't want it and won't read it, but it's brand new
- ❑ Salvaged—saved from extinction, for what reason is still not clear
- ❑ Book club book—by-default shelf-filler
- ❑ Decorator—book kept to impress onlookers/intellectuals
- ❑ Blinded by the binding—books with beautiful leather bindings and pages that will never be cracked

After sorting, proceed to one of the following:

- Dump, sell, recycle
- Reroute to someone who cares
- Strip or rip out the few pages that were all you really wanted anyway
- READ—dust it off, read it, and keep it for the whole family to enjoy

Always determine "shelf life" yourself. Only you know your book needs, wants, and wishes. Once your library is "culled," purged and purified, you can savor what you have. This also saves dusting, and forever criticizing yourself for "never getting at those books."

GOAL:

Some book breathing room in your mind and in your mansion. Easy access to your good and beloved books, and room for new, better books coming into your life.

For more on taking a hard look at books, see Chapter 8 of *Clutter's Last Stand* and *Not for Packrats Only*, and Chapter 6 of *Clutter Free! Finally and Forever*.

They say that the shelf life of new books in a bookstore now is often only about two weeks—maybe we should be more like this.

"Apart from a few favorite cookbooks, well and often used, I only save individual recipes (and only those which have been tried and tested and found worthy of repeated use). These slip easily into plastic sleeves that I keep in a binder. I have an index at the front which I update every couple of years (a ten-minute task). I even (gasp!) slice the page I want right out of a cookbook to keep, and give away the book."

ENTERTAIN-MENT Clutter

(The most modern clutter.)
Unwanted, broken, or obsolete TVs, VCRs, sound systems, boom boxes, instruments, videotapes, video games, audio cassettes, CD's, records, earphones, antennas, speakers, programs, performance debris, cards, games, puzzles, and other adult pacifiers, and the biggest junk bunkers of all, entertainment centers.

SUMMARY:

This is one of the rights we, the modern generation, have added to the Constitution, the right to be entertained—the need or desire to be amused is gaining on the sex and hunger drives. We of course look for that entertainment from the outside instead of the inside and so have equipped our homes, cars, buildings, and body with devices to feed us sounds and sensations to get us through the day. The original "one radio for entertainment" has grown to an entire wall of the home, in which is installed every entertainment device imaginable, almost letting media make our lives.

SOLUTION:

Cut down the volume of intake of all those "too much" entertainments. Use entertainment to refresh yourself, not occupy all your free time.

Balance what you have by way of entertainment equipment and what you need. If you don't use something, sell it or give it away.

Face up to the music or other fun stuff (records, tapes, etc.) you ran to the register with, but don't really dig. Dump any "base" stuff you aren't really proud to own, and sell or donate the rest.

If parts are no longer available, it would cost a small fortune to repair, or there's no way of getting rid of the static on it, do you really still want it?? Try not to buy tapes you haven't heard, rent rather than buy movies you aren't going to watch often again, and avoid joining music or video clubs.

GOAL:

Find entertainment within yourself, so you won't have to keep tuning in and out.

For more on tuning out entertainment clutter, see p. 102 of *Clutter's Last Stand*, and p. 75 of *Not for Packrats Only*.

SUMMARY:

This clutter is strictly personal and is viewed as a vital operational tool—the resources we need to make it through the average day. But a good forty percent of this carry-along clutter could be done without, and makes for a far bigger load to lug than we want or need.

All of this weight makes us look and feel like a pack mule, for what?

SOLUTION:

Spread all of your carry-around clutter out on the bed so you can weigh it mentally and physically. This will convince you this has to be the silliest of all excess, clutter that you haul around with you every day and hour. Your goal, even if you keep all the categories of stuff you see here, is to reduce the weight by at least a third. Cut six credit cards down to two, get rid of all obsolete keys and leave the seldom-used ones home, dump any unnecessary drugs, weed down that grooming gear, go to smaller versions of everything, condense, miniaturize, drop those pennies in the piggybank, move to a smaller wallet or purse. Review everything (from wallet photos to lucky charms to insurance and library cards) for long out of date stuff. This is one area of clutter only YOU can deal with, and you can and should show some guts. Purge those purses and pockets!

CARRY-ALONG Clutter

Contents of wallets, pockets, purses, cosmetic cases, briefcases—photos, puzzles, keys, keychains, checkbooks, address books, writing gear, planners, cards, tickets, coupons, coins, tokens, grooming tools, cosmetics, good luck charms, nibbles, breath sweeteners, drugs, cameras, clothes, weather protection gear and personal protection gear.

GOAL:

The goal is to travel light,* be 100 percent up to date, and not have to feel or slap your pockets or rummage for even a second when you need something, or are asked for something.

*Unless you have a baby. You are excused for up to 30 pounds of infant stuff—necessities and accessories.

For more on jettisoning carry-along clutter see page 158 of *Clutter's Last Stand*, Chapter 7 of *Not for Packrats Only*, and Chapters 3 and 4 of *The Office Clutter Cure*.

FITNESS Clutter

Jogging shoes, running shoes, aerobic shoes, socks with pompoms, vitamin bottles, water bottles (and straws and belt loops and packs for same), treadmills, pads and mats, benches and belts, and tables, weights of all kinds, bags and totes of every shape and description, t-shirts from every marathon, walk or competition, special bras and straps and jox and sox, knee braces, wrist supports and back supports, magic stretchers and squeezers, springs, sweatsuits, sweatbands, hip and tummy reducers, bust builders, punching bags, exercycles, video workouts from every major supermodel and star.

SUMMARY:

One of the fastest-multiplying forms of modern-day clutter. We buy the latest and the greatest, but hang on to every old club and racquet, too. Motivated by the latest studies on cholesterol or calorie consumption, or a look in the mirror, we go hog wild getting tools, machines, gear and gadgets of all kinds, books and videos to get in shape. Most of which are soon stashed in the closet, under the bed, or in the basement. But we keep buying new ones. The other day I saw a fellow carrying a new Nordic track exercise machine into his house, walking right past the hired guys mowing his lawn. The only real exercise that results from many of these machines is the extra walking you have to do to step around them, the effort involved in moving them from room to room (trying to find somewhere out of the way to keep them), cleaning around them, and the extra hours you have to work to pay for them. The only thing in the house getting stronger is the floor and walls, from the weight of these anti-weight machines. Most people have fitness clutter all over the house and most people don't use it.

SOLUTION:

1. Eat less.

2. Buy used stuff so you can easily jettison it when it doesn't work or you get tired of it.

3. Get a second job lifting grain sacks somewhere.

4. Jog or walk rather than saunter. Use the streets and parks, instead of your house to exercise, and there will be zero need for stuff.

5. Buy a new shovel or rake and use it.

6. I can't think of any other solutions for fitness clutter because I believe it is a total waste of time and money.

GOAL:

Just keeping our house and yard in shape will generally keep us in shape without the tons of fitness trappings and paraphernalia.

For more on freeing yourself of fitness clutter, see Chapters 6 and 7 of *Not for Packrats Only*.

SUMMARY:

The more "sporty" we become, the more we multiply our trappings as new and better and recommended-by-the-professionals come along. But sports are often a brief phase of life or a passing fancy. We are into something briefly, our children briefly, then we are in it as spectators. (Meaning that all the gear that made us go, could probably go now.)

SOLUTION:

1. When you lose your enthusiasm for something, donate it to the kids on the block. There is always a new and needy generation of fresh, eager youth to literally "fill your shoes."

2. If something means a great deal to you still, though you're not using it, mount it. If there is a jersey, ball, bat, fishing rod, or one or two other treasures in the sports pile that hold hero memories which you just cannot let go—good! Find a way to mount it on a plaque or a frame. Then hang it up and savor it while the crowd cheers again silently.

3. Store it: Much athletics or sports gear that's had its day, is in the way. It might be used again if it can be contained and at least gotten out of our everyday way. Big plastic tubs are great for this, they sure beat broken field running plays to try and find "it" when you want it.

GOAL:

Is to still be a sport when necessary, but not wade in sports fallout

SPORTS Clutter

Balls, bats, mitts, racquets, cleats, helmets, shoes, jerseys, hats, hats, hats, more hats, glasses, socks, tackle boxes, maps, lures, nets, strings, float tubes and appendages, guns, shells, knives, boots, tents, stoves, bandages, uniforms, packs, cameras, photos, trophies, braces, gloves, shin guards, wrist braces, elbow and knee pads, mouthpieces, goggles, magazines, canteens, pads, vests, floats, boats, skis, poles, parkas.

forever. The sports equipment you do use or want to keep should be easily accessible. And what you've outgrown should go—somewhere—this weekend.

For more on clearing the field of sports clutter, see Chapter 7 of *Not for Packrats Only*, p. 114 of *Clutter Free!*, and p. 111-112 of *Clutter's Last Stand*.

"I use my treadmill in the bedroom to hang my extra clothes on."

PAPER Clutter

Letters, junk mail, notes, reports, memos, ads, brochures, fliers, files, photocopies, clippings, receipts, catalogs, cards, envelopes, bills, magazines, newspapers, newsletters, warranties and instructions, etc.

SUMMARY:

We probably process (or should) 200-400 sheets of paper per day, and the number is only increasing. All that paper piles up and it turns us into diggers and hunters, it makes us late, takes up space, hurts our image, and confuses us. It breeds indecision and blocks relationships. And it doesn't self-destruct. Paper weight, once a nice little knickknack, is now a general condition.

SOLUTION:

Number one: The daily paper stream. The key is to CONDENSE it as soon as it comes in:

The fresh arrivals…

Keepers…

For more on shearing through paper clutter, see Chapter 8 of *Clutter's Last Stand* and *Not for Packrats Only*, Chapter 6 of *Clutter Free! Finally and Forever*, and *The Office Clutter Cure*.

Number Two: The backlog. Sort it quickly into 4 categories:

OUT

The awful, the obsolete, the empty, the un-understandable, the uninteresting, the unneeded. TOSS, HAVE TRANSLATED, OR RECYCLE IT!

ROUTE

Stuff that is out of place, belongs to others, should go to a different department, or be moved to storage. SEND TO SOMEONE OR SOMEPLACE ELSE.

DOUBT

Things to read, to answer, to process, to think over. TAKE WITH YOU TO DIGEST. And deal with them the moment you do!

SPROUT

Your good ideas, your dream project, long-lost documents, leads, and addresses, etc. FILE SO YOU CAN FIND THEM.

GOAL:

Working space!!! Being ahead, not behind, able to locate things instantly, no apologizing anymore. Reclaiming one hundred percent of that time lost rummaging and hunting.

SUMMARY:

They served well once, and if they can do so again, great! But keeping every single one of them on your payroll "until you need them" is often a cost higher than the purchase of nice new enclosures. Packaging clutter is a prime fire, rodent, roach, and termite hazard, and who really has a place to keep packaging clutter? When we do need a container to ship or repackage something, our chances of finding something that fits in the midst of all this are almost nil. (Claiming these are "craft supplies" is no excuse.)

SOLUTION:

Selectivity is the key here. It makes both environmental and economic sense to have some containers around, for mailing, storing, or carrying things, or to send other junk away in. So:

- First eliminate all the defective stuff—flimsy and sawed off-boxes, the water-damaged, crushed, mildewed, and rat-chewed ones. The holey sacks, rusty cans, dented tins, etc.
- Pick out the "primo" containers and put them to work, right now.
- Then take about half the amount of containers you think you will need in the future and put them back in storage inside each other. But this time locate them in such a way that they don't take up important central storage space, and so that you can find them when you need

PACKAGING Clutter

Boxes, wrappers, bags, plastic sacks, empty Cool Whip containers (the queen of container clutter), jugs, bottles, cookie tins, bubble pack, "ghost droppings" (Styrofoam peanuts), freezer pak, crates, egg cartons, foil, pie tins, mailing enclosures of any kind, and yes even those lovely reinforced computer boxes.

them. Just keep one or two boxes of cardboard boxes, stacked inside each other. Cardboard boxes can be stored much more efficiently if you break them down, but putting them back together is a pain.
- Recycle, trash, or burn all the rest.
- Getting in the fling of it as new boxes and bags flow in will help keep the packaging stream under control. You can also share the extras with friends and neighbors who are "looking for boxes for a move," and the like.

GOAL:

Not keeping any used packaging around that doesn't have an honest chance of being reused.

For more on packing out packaging clutter, see Chapter 8 of *Not for Packrats Only* and Chapter 6 of *Clutter Free! Finally and Forever*.

SENTIMENTAL Stuff

Keepsakes, charms, corsages, souvenirs, diaries, ribbons, letters, notes, poems, awards, jewelry, antiques, locks of hair, dishes, cups, collections, homemade items, broken valuables, coins, parts, programs, clippings, clothing, photos, school papers, scrapbooks, trophies... this is a never-ending list!

SUMMARY:

Much of this IS valuable, because things like this can be the anchors of posterity, the markers of a trail (or trial) you don't want to lose or forget. Keeping a token can keep a memory alive. Sentiment is one of the most valuable of virtues, it preserves a thread of human decency we'd all be lost without. But when you start feeling sorry for sentimental stuff, or keeping it begins to punish you instead of give you pleasure, it's time to point your compassion in a better direction.

SOLUTION:

Give your sentimental stuff the old 1-2:

1. CULL—Time takes a toll on sentimental stuff—we outlive and outgrow a lot of it. It served its time well, it is ready for pardon, so release it. If not only the item but the memories it held are faded and worn (or simply something you'd now like to forget), let it go.

If you find this hard to do, have any lingering doubts about a particular piece of sentimental savings, you can photograph it, or miniaturize it. Clip just one button off that old moth-eaten sweater, or a bit of the lace trim from that old camisole before you drop it in the dumpster or charity collection bin.

2. ACTIVATE—You kept it for a reason, to show it, stroke it, be inspired by it. So now do it, get some value out of those valuables. Find a way to make them active instead of passively stored in a trunk or shed somewhere. Reposition them, repaint them, revive them. Convert them to something you can use in everyday life—mount them, frame them, hang them, move them to somewhere you can see and enjoy them, share them, maybe even flaunt them. They need to be in action, not in a hole somewhere.

You might also want to label them clearly for easy identification by your heirs.

GOAL:

Weed it down to what really matters, and then make it part of your life!

For more on coming to terms with sentimental clutter, see Chapter 7 of *Clutter's Last Stand*, Chapter 8 of *Not for Packrats Only*, and Chapter 6 of *Clutter Free! Finally and Forever*.

SUMMARY:

We've got it all… waiting for parts, time to fix it, a miraculous recovery, or a mate, neighbor, or talented son-in-law to come help us "heal" it. We feel guilt or sympathy for these things in their present condition, that is one reason we still have them. We forget, all too easily, that if it doesn't work it isn't working for us. We are working for it—storing it, explaining it, shuffling it from place to place. A big part of our excess pounds of objects, and our mental load, is on this "to be repaired" list.

SOLUTION:

Own nothing that doesn't work, or is wounded. Fix it now or find a different future for it.

The "FIXABLES"

Things that aren't working, broken things, things with parts missing, things that are obsolete, dull, out of tune, cracked, frozen, scorched, rusted, chipped, stained, rotted, rodentized. Plus "the old one" from anything we did fix.

For more on facing down "gonna fix it" clutter, see Chapter 5 of *Clutter's Last Stand*, Chapter 7 of *Not for Packrats Only*, and Chapters 3 and 4 of *The Office Clutter Cure*.

REPAIR CHECKLIST

IS IT HONESTLY FIXABLE?

YES	NO	
☐	☐	Will I use it again when it's fixed, and for what?
☐	☐	Are parts and refills really available for it?
☐	☐	Can I really fix this myself (do I have the talent and time)?
☐	☐	Is there a convenient/expert place to have it repaired?
☐	☐	Will the end results justify the cost of fixing: labor, parts, shipping, phone bills, driving time, the search to find someone who can fix it, having a second person work on it after the first one fails to fix it, etc.?
☐	☐	Do I have a nonoffensive place to keep it until it's fixed?

GOAL:

Ridding, or restoration.

SOMEDAY Stuff

Partly done projects, unopened kits, furniture to finish, restore, or haul off, old carpets we meant to put down somewhere, letters and books to finish, good intentions unacted upon, apologies unmade, trips or visits we wanted to make, aged chemicals, paint, seeds, things to wear or to try someday; piles of things marked "To the Kids," "To Be Recycled," or "To the Dump"—all sitting in the cellar, attic, junk room, or shed, waiting on YOU.

SUMMARY:

Someday stuff is the champion of the scale tilters, the real heavy. What is it? The kept but unfinished, the good intentions, the hopes and ambitions withered on the vine. Some of this might still deserve its day, but has died or is dying waiting for it.

SOLUTION:
(Caution—can cause delight or depression.)

We are going to determine how many days you actually have left to deal with someday stuff. Sit down and calculate the number of years you have left on this earth (the average man lives approximately 74 years, the average woman 80). Multiply that by 52, the number of weeks in a year, and it will make you think in a perspective you never have. I have only five hundred and twenty weeks

left here. "Someday" doesn't stretch on forever—making someday TODAY is the solution. After you've narrowed those piles and stacks down to the stuff you do still really want to get to, you know what to do, so start doing it TODAY!

GOAL:

The reward for weeding down all that someday stuff: room for tomorrow!

For more on calling the bluff of "do it someday" stuff, see Chapter 5 of *Clutter's Last Stand*, Chapter 7 of *Not for Packrats Only*, and Chapter 6 of *Clutter Free! Finally and Forever*.

SUMMARY:

This dropped off, left behind, forgotten, or intentionally-stored-there stuff is someone else's to worry about and look after. (And it takes up and junks up their precious ROOM, too.) It is unkind, obnoxious, inconsiderate, immoral even, to leave our litter somewhere too long. Offering short-term storage to someone until they can reload or relocate is true charity, but this dislocated clutter gets old fast for those housing it, whether family, friends, or enemies! The worse the junk, the worse the irritation. Good family and friends will keep (neatly boxed) good stuff longer, but don't forget about it and don't forget to thank them.

SOLUTION:

Make a written list or chart of your invasions:

FARMED OUT Weight

It's yours, all right, but it's not at your place! Clothes, cars, containers of clutter of all kinds, kept or left at someone else's place.

GOAL:

Not to let stuff we have stashed anywhere wear out its welcome (or for that matter, ours!)

INVENTORY

WHAT	WHERE IS IT	WHY	SINCE WHEN	DISPOSITION
Maternity/ baby stuff	At Mother's	Since we moved	20 years ago	I'm 65—guess I can give it away
My Ford Falcon	The vacant lot at work	Transmission finally went	6 months ago	Call the junk dealer today!

If you are shocked by the first four columns above, activate that last one right away. Too many of us shunt our "too much" onto others.

For more on "mother load" clutter, see Chapter 7 of *Not for Packrats Only*, and Chapter 6 of *Clutter Free! Finally and Forever*.

FOR SALE

REAL ESTATE Clutter

Extra land, lawn, home space, sheds, apartments, time shares, vacation homes, speculation properties... that you don't use.

SUMMARY:

We don't want all the land in the world, just all that borders us! Too many of us end up (through inheritance, remodeling, moving, upgrading, idle coveting, or just plain building a life and family or business) with "too much" property or land, which we hang on to for dear life. Take buildings, for instance. What once housed a family or earned a living is great, but when we outgrow it or no longer need something quite so big, it often stays to be cared for (cleaned and maintained and policed and taxed, etc.). Shelter can evolve to something to shepherd, and excess land can easily become a preburial plot for us.

SOLUTION:

For landlock:

List or lay out on paper ALL the properties you own and honestly enter their status and forecast below.

In forty years of being responsible for real estate, I've owned a bunch of it, and the answer is to move it when and if you're not using it or don't have a clear projected plan for it. Keeping property for investment purposes or enjoyment makes sense, but not keeping it just because you have it. Realtors will tell you that, too. The basis for judgment here is whether it is a delight and pleasure, a positive influence on you and others—or a drain. When you can't ride your range, put it to rest.

REAL ESTATE CODE (GOAL):

Not letting land or property put you under.

For more real estate reading, see pages 91, 94, and 201 of *Clutter's Last Stand*, and page 61 of *Not for Packrats Only*.

After the initial euphoria of owning two homes wears off, most people wake up to the reality that now they have two places to mind and maintain. Now they have to keep two places in order, and worry about the preservation and condition of two. And now they have double everything to do before they can take off on a trip anywhere.

PARCEL OR PROPERTY	ORIG. COST	TODAY'S VALUE	TAXES	PAYMENTS	INTEREST	TIME PERIOD	MAINTENANCE COSTS	(REALISTIC) FUTURE VALUE

SUMMARY:

We've built our fleet, in less than eighty years, from a mere means of transportation to vehicles that ease work and provide sport, romance, and excitement. There is a vehicle to fit almost every phase of our life, work, play, and ego. They're easy to buy, too, so even a person of modest means can easily end up with several vehicles to tend. Once the average person owned a two-ton car. Now automobiles are smaller and lighter, but we often have two or more of them apiece. Maintaining all this—making the payments on them, insuring, protecting, cleaning and polishing them, and finding a place to park and store them (plus guilt about the ones we don't use enough to justify ownership of)—is weight indeed.

SOLUTION:

Vehicle clutter has two basic causes:

Too many cars

Spare shoes or hand tools are hard enough to tend, but a spare vehicle that gets limited or little use depreciates you even faster than it. Infrequently used vehicles, vehicles that were once used and now are not, "I'm going to restore/repair/rebuild it someday" vehicles, and plain old junk cars around your place, your folks' place, the storage center, the lot next door, or the back forty is nothing but clutter on wheels.

Too much car

Luxury is a silly word to connect with cars. Safety and soundness are

VEHICLE Clutter

Cars, trucks, vans, jeeps, RV's, sports cars, go-karts, three-wheelers, fifth wheels, motorcycles, motorbikes, snowmobiles, trailers, boats, tanks, tractors, "restorable," "repairable," and retired vehicles.

one thing, but luxury (that $10,000, $20,000, or $30,000 extra you pay for exclusive transportation) is weight indeed, and expensive no matter how ingeniously you finance it. Is the few hours or minutes you spend daily in a car worth weeks and years of straining and stretching to pay for it? Or the loss of the better things you could do with that money? Vanity is one of life's largest weights and vehicles reign as one of the top vanity victimizers (of men, especially).

The average car today can get you where you want and need to go, look neat and presentable, and be safe for 100,000 to 200,000 miles, even 300,000 miles. Keeping your present car as long as you can will save money, time, and the environment.

GOAL:

To be in the "driver's seat" again. Trading all that parking space for some room for personal growth.

For more on minimizing vehicle clutter, see Chapter 10 of *Clutter's Last Stand*, Chapter 6 of *Not for Packrats Only*, and Chapter 6 of *Clutter Free! Finally and Forever*.

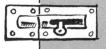

PROTECTIVE Clutter

Locks, keys, alarms, monitors, buzzers, guards, bars, fences, electric eyes, closed-circuit TV, security lights, safes, safe deposit boxes, insurance on car, house, contents, and person (and insurance inventories), Mace, tear gas, guard dogs, guns.

SUMMARY:

It's a real irony, isn't it, that we strive and save to buy a bunch of "good stuff," and then have so many expensive things we need to own, rent, or lease a string of alarms, locks, safes, fences, guards, and electronics to protect them, because we aren't there using them. All this protection gear takes up space and it has to be installed, maintained, monitored, kept records on, and paid for, for what? To guard our "too much." People seldom steal the common everyday necessities—it's the luxury stuff that is always the target. The jewels or the paintings are too expensive to wear or show, so we hide them, and pay for protectors to keep not us, but our stuff out of danger. The result is that we spend about a quarter of our lives getting in and out of places or areas at work and at home.

SOLUTION:

Protection devices create more tension than peace of mind, as one is always worried about whether they are working right, and whether we have the best or right one.

The best **self-protection** (which is our ultimate goal) is having less possessions people want to take from you. So walk through your inventory and list just what-all you are "guarding," and then beside each listed item write—**why**. If the why is honestly good, it's a keeper. If you have to think or ask why twice, it is generally something you might consider finding a new owner for.

GOAL:

Culling those "valuables" down to the things that are truly valuable **to you**. Carrying less keys, combinations, codes, and concealed apparatuses, having less code numbers, lights, and locks to worry about.

For more on security clutter, see page 51 of *Clutter's Last Stand*.

SUMMARY:

Although the garage is often the largest open space on the home scene, it is the least wisely used. Seldom can a car get in. The garage offers us space for active and creative projects and we offer it our piles of pathetic house and yard overflow. Truly this is the "on its way out, but detained for further study" syndrome. Most garages offer an obstacle course of opportunities to trip and fall, plus a place for things to rot or receive damage. And a sure source of a heated argument or two (or more).

SOLUTION:

First: Simply, honestly, remove all the TRASH! Things that are:

- Empty
- Dried up
- Hardened
- Broken
- Outdated
- Worn out
- Bottomless
- Unfixable
- Rejected (you never wanted it, or you have a better one)

Second: Restore or reroute the rest:

- Sharpen the dull
- Paint the ugly, peeling, or porous
- Return the borrowed or pirated, and call the owners of anything else that isn't yours and tell them it's time for pickup
- Relocate the things that don't fit here or belong somewhere else
- Refinish or repair things in need of it, and move them back into the house

Third: Mount or cover anything you can. Any way you can get "it" (a worthwhile, legitimate garage inhabitant) off the floor, do it—shelve it, wall hang it, put in a closet or cabinet.

GARAGE Junk

Parts, accessories, and attachments to all kinds of things, construction scraps/leftovers, chemicals, broken items, seasonal stuff, trash and garbage, gardening goodies, cleaning gear, oils, solvents, and rags, every tool coming and going, recycling inventory, drums and containers, second-best furniture, retired cars.

Clear off that concrete!

Fourth: Seal the floor.

Buy a can of clear concrete seal. Clean and prepare the floor following the instructions on the can, and then coat the entire floor with seal and let it dry well. This will give you a shiny, smooth surface to drive, walk, and work on. Pet droppings, oil drips, and spills can be removed, and project mess swept up, in seconds.

The garage is the first area you see when you get home and the most direct route into your house. When clean, it will not only give you a lift, but prevent stains and litter from drifting into the house.

GOAL:

To have room for the car, and to do projects, without having to clear away and rearrange things.

For more on de-garbaging the garage, see p. 92-93 of *Clutter's Last Stand*, p. 82-83 of *Make Your House Do the Housework*, page 60 of *Not for Packrats Only*, and page 145-146 of *Clutter Free: Finally and Forever*.

OUTDOOR clutter

Parked or porched toys, tools, tires, rusted iron and steel, scraps and torn-out stuff from remodeling jobs and do-it-yourself projects, old flowerpots and potting supplies, abandoned vehicles and vehicle parts, bags and sacks, rotting firewood, old doghouses, defunct bird feeders, sagging swing sets, leaning sheds, failing fences, dead lawn mowers and appliances, litter and garbage, deteriorated yard decorations, dead bushes, fallen tree branches, parts, more parts, packaging, evicted furniture.

SUMMARY:

First impressions, and even final judgments about our character and housekeeping are made before anyone ever meets us or enters our home. Our grounds give us away and can keep respect, pride, and efficiency away, too. Trash outside hints at trash inside. Mother Nature is not going to remove most of this!

SOLUTION:

Contain

Have nothing out or loose that can show, get wet, or blow around, nothing attractive to thieves or dangerous to children. Just have the real usables and the weatherproof out there. Keep dust and mud-producing dirt covered with vegetation, and dead or broken parts of trees and bushes pruned.

Refrain

The yard is not a place to stash or store things. Weather and exposure take a big toll, so anything outside has an ongoing price tag with a big "TO DO" on it. Limit what you put out here, and you won't have to be constantly painting, repainting, covering up, taking in and out, retrieving, tying down, etc.

Maintain

Trade your exercise equipment for an active yard care/scouting session. Grounds need regular policing to remain unjunked.

GOAL:

Not having to endure—coming or going—anything resembling an obstacle course. Eliminating any visual pollution, as well as the need to make excuses or apologies for the condition of our grounds. Making any outside space we own an attractive place to play ball, sniff flowers, or roll downhill.

For more on ousting outdoor clutter, see Chapters 5, 6, and 12 of *Clutter's Last Stand*, Chapters 6 and 7 of *Not for Packrats Only*, and pages 137-138 of *Clutter Free! Finally & Forever.*

SUMMARY:

One kid today has more stuff than an entire kindergarten a few years ago. The source of all this is both heredity and environment, or in other words, us—the adults of all ages who lugged all this in and laid it on our kids. (All the while, humming our theme song, "Be good and Mommy/ Daddy will bring you home some _____[junk].") A very high percentage of kiddie clutter is things bought to please and appease kids, often as a substitute for time spent with them. The choice here is to lose the clutter, or you'll lose the kid (in more ways than one) in it.

SOLUTION:

1. **GIVE IT A PLACE:** Kids' stuff, especially, needs to have a designated area, to be containable. If there isn't a specific place or space to park it when the playing is over for the day, then out with it. Overflow will always be underfoot.

2. **DE-DUPLICATE:** Double and triple of everything is a great way to spoil kids and teach them indecision and waste. And remember that replacing any broken thing, refilling every toy vacancy, is not a child-raising requirement.

3. **RETREAT:** From offers of extra gifts, and trips and places that have a big take-home souvenir price tag.

KIDS' Clutter

Papers, crayons, stuffed animals, play sets, cribs, chairs, fast food fallout, balls, bats, strollers, kiddie care gear and car gear, books, dolls, pets, toys, toys, toys, toyboxes. There are at least 6,000 categories of child clutter!

GOAL:

To save our children, rather than all that stuff that will only spoil and confuse them, or warp their values. Their hands can be better occupied than with a joystick, and where there is less clutter there will be less nagging, yelling, arguing, and little kiddie fights.

For more on controlling kiddie clutter, see page 90 of *Clutter's Last Stand*, Chapter 15 of *Not for Packrats Only*, and Chapter 6 of *Clutter Free! Finally and Forever*.

PET Clutter

Cages, collars, leashes, chains, toys, tags, dishes and feeders and leftover food by the broken sack, pills, powders, and pharmaceutical potions, kitty beds and doggie quilts, grooming tools, pedigrees, training aids, shampoos, leads, saddles, harnesses, chains, litter handling devices, stained containers, and abandoned aquariums complete with mossy castles, blue gravel, and broken pump.

SUMMARY:

Pets are meant to bless, not mess up our lives. The time, space, and money to keep pets and all of their paraphernalia is well spent if they give us pleasure. (And there are pets whose personality surpasses that of most humans in the household.) The "burden" of pets is often not them but all the excess trappings and supplies we accumulate while the pet is with us, or keep long after the pet is gone. Active articles are all right, it is the obsolete, the duplicates, the nonused, and the nonworking that become the tail that wags the dog.

SOME DOGGONE GOOD SOLUTIONS:

- Centralizing pet supplies and accessories (and maybe even the pets themselves) to "their room

or area" of the house and grounds can do a lot to cut down pet clutter.

- Trash (or sell or pass on) all the duplicates, ruined, outgrown, or retired things, and the "didn't work" or "wouldn't eat" items.
- Don't keep paraphernalia for pets you're no longer interested in, or if both the pet and those who loved the pet are gone!
- Point out the burden of pet overload to the owner of the pet, if it happens to not be you.
- Resist ever **getting** a pet that you aren't going to **stay** interested in, and be willing to take the time and trouble to take care of.

GOAL:

Something to bark, crow, and chirp about—less pet mess. You'll have more room for Rover, less stain and odor, less hunting for things, and fewer heated discussions.

For more on minimizing pet mess, see page 264 of *Clutter's Last Stand*, page 88 of *Not for Packrats Only*, and *Pet Clean-Up Made Easy*—a fun guide to every aspect of pet mess cleanup and prevention.

SUMMARY:

Things like this, we often don't even know why we are keeping— maybe on a dare, to irritate someone else, because we are not 100 percent sure what it is, or maybe it has been the only thing we can spark conversation with. Or maybe we just never thought about it.

Stupid stuff is really of no use or value to anyone (including us), and it may even give us bad vibes. Yet we have kept it and are still keeping it. It doesn't have a chance of becoming an antique, it's not even good for a laugh anymore. One or two stupid things keep us human and humble, the other forty-six are pushing us toward imbecile qualification.

SOLUTION:

- This is one case where it is okay to let others express their opinion of your junk, and you listen to them.
- Pass stupid stuff on to a new generation of jokers, if they show any interest in it.
- Display and offer it at a "stupid party" (especially if drinks are being served).
- You can, of course, just TRASH it!

GOAL:

Keep only the stuff that has some class, or some purpose. Make sure anything of this type that you keep has some redeeming value for you or others, and that you do have the space to accommodate it (stupid space).

REAL STUPID Stuff

Kidney stone pendant, ex-husband's toenail, wad of stuck-together Green Stamps, twenty years' worth of wishbones, dead cactus complete with pot, bale of hay in basement, your ex-wife's back brace, leopard-skin covered water heater made into a chair, a pirated "No U Turn" sign, the cast that was removed from your cat's broken leg, crate of cordova shoe polish, bladeless fan, bald snow tires, blackened, broken baby tooth, pet snake's shed skin, raunchy old raccoon hide, purse made out of an armadillo, shelf ornament made out of a moose dropping, half-melted mushroom-shaped candle. I think you get the idea.

For more secrets of shucking real stupid stuff, see any chapter of my four other books on dejunking.

OTHERS' clutter

Anything covered in this book, except it is someone else's, not yours. Habits, hardware, soft goods, or general mess.

SUMMARY:

A number of people have written me over the years about how their mother or father or friend, etc., "does not see the mess" that they are living in. It may be total chaos and squalor, and yet they see absolutely nothing amiss.

> *"I've begun to declutter in spite of my husband's valiant effort to protect 60 pairs of shoes, 84 pairs of socks, 75 collected caps, and sets of 1936 law books…. I'm not perfect, but compared to him…."*

When someone else's stuff is out of control, it often goes out of bounds and infringes on our territory—affects our nerves, pocketbook, and flexibility. We end up carrying some of their weight and we don't like it. Until they lose their excess, we in subtle or not so subtle ways are abused and embarrassed by it (people may avoid visiting, make sarcastic comments, etc.). This is not something we want to face forever—we'll do it for ours, but not for theirs. And we prefer not to use the rock-bottom alternatives, such as leaving, torching the pile, or getting a divorce.

SOLUTION:

None of the following work, so save your energy:

Threatening, intimidating, nagging, criticizing, serving notice, preaching, plundering their stash, or demanding that they get rid of all this, or else! Even when something is cursed and disliked by the owner himself, just try to take it away from him and you would think he was losing his birthright.

What does work?

- Let them know (in a low-key, loving way) that you really don't like it.
- Limit their area. Most people respect boundaries when they're clearly spelled out. Confine the space and you'll confine the stuff.
- Be a perfect example of clutter-free living yourself. Say by actions (NOT words!): "Look at all the room I have, Harry."
- The most effective approach is and always will be good example. Exposing someone long and subtly enough to a squared-

away life will eventually, in due time, ignite a spark of understanding that living clutter-free is living better. And when they do alter their cluttering course, they'll know what to do because of what they have seen.

- Praise, admore, and compliment any improvements they make.
- Avoid cluttered situations and people in the first place.

GOAL:

To somehow motivate them to clear away the clutter so you can find eacher, often for the first time!

For more sane solutions to others' clutter, see Chapters 14 and 16 of *Not for Packrats Only*, and Chapter 6 of *Clutter Free! Finally & Forever*, and pages 96-97 of *The Office Clutter Cure*.

"One thing that is helping the cause is including my husband in the dejunking decisions. He's still a pack-rat, but I think all he wanted in the past was to be in the loop. I'll fill up a box and show it to him. It's amazing how little he actually pulls out to keep. And this is the man who stashed a lawnmower in our living room several years ago."

Needed! Inventions and tools to assist clutter sufferers:

- *Pile X Ray*
- *Clutter carbon dater (as the little prongs or suction cups make contact, it analyzes, ages, weighs, and dates things)*
- *Clutter wallpaper (you can see and savor it all, but not have to dust it or deal with it in any way)*
- *A bottomless shopping bag*

CHAPTER 6

To Keep It Off Now!

Preventing future clutter: the most important step of all!

You know how a yo-yo works, a little round object that goes away and then comes speeding right back to you? Well, this happens with weight loss, too—millions of Americans go on a diet each year, and then, regardless of how "successful" they were, gain 90 percent of that extra flesh back within five years. That's a pretty bleak outlook for any weight on us, but the clutter picture is actually even worse. When it comes to a clutter diet (which at least as many of us go on each year), if we're not careful within five years we'll have not 90 percent, but 150 percent of that excess back in our bins again.

So our final success in losing the 200 pounds this weekend is tied to what we do—or don't—pick back up the next weekend.

"You asked how my house decluttering was going? I killed the beast, only to find out it had resurrected. Yes, I've learned that whatever I feed will grow!"

"I bought a farmhouse from a woman of seventy-five, and it was filled with junk—balls of string, empty plastic bags, and tons of other stuff. It took a full year to get it cleaned out. I was horrified the whole time. The most horrible thing, however, was that within three months I had totally refilled it (and I moved there from an apartment)."

One of the biggest problems with those hell-bent to live free of junk and clutter is that they make dejunking a one-night stand—slam, bam, thank you garbage can. Then they forget clutter until it starts again to fester. Losing is about half of this 200 pounds project; keeping it lost is the other half. Clutter is not an "I got rid of it" process, it is more like AA: "I'm a clutteraholic, surrounded and tempted by it hourly, if not every second."

Slipping back into clutter after we've overcome it is just as awful as going back to hitting the bottle, nursing a cigarette, or gnawing on our cuticles. Sliding back, regaining old discarded habits, habits we were very happy to be relieved of, really hurts. Need I say more? So let's not even consider refilling our garage, drawers, closets, and catacombs once we've decluttered them. Kids are smart enough not to play again with the dog that bit them, let us be as wise.

So what can we do to KEEP clutter gone, now?

Don't just weed it out, get rid of it

Make sure that when you say goodbye to junk it's a clean, clear, definite "Goodbye," not "See you later, stuffed alligator."

"Going" is seldom as good as "gone."

Operate current

Don't let things pile up, gaining is slow but sure (and gruesome). Keep active stuff, shun the passive.

Actively dodge and avoid clutter

One thing about those pounds of ugly extra, nowadays we don't have to go after them, because of that magic business buzzword called marketing. Every other time we pick up the phone, we find ourselves being talked, by some determined person, into a product or service that was nowhere on our list of things to look into next. Catalogs for things we don't need and wouldn't have sought out jam our mailboxes, and TV and radio are full of dramatic ads for more. Door-to-door solicitors, amateur and professional, and friends pushing some line of products accost us every time we turn around.

The bottom line is you can't just be a passive dejunker these days, you've got to be actively alert for clutter, constantly dodging and avoiding it. Too much doesn't arrive all at once. Clutter is rarely the result of one big event or one big mistake. It comes in a little at a time: a little

picking up of little things at little shops for little reasons… total up to BIG results in the end, a lot of extra weight around the house.

As one man put it, "I can't remember buying more than a few suits, and I have forty-one suits now, and that's not counting the ones at the other house." Stay alert and on your guard: every little act and purchase counts!

A home full of clutter (like love or hate, wealth or poverty, leadership or following) is the result of many efforts, decisions, and actions over time. Clutter is like a glacier—you never see its mass move, but eventually it quietly smothers all in its path.

Think before you buy or charge

"Why did I do that?" We ask ourselves this question a lot, don't we? Even me—I'm well educated, street smart, steeped in the subject of clutter, fully aware of the sins of others, and a great giver of advice. Last month, I visited a major city on a convention trip. I already have a dozen sweatshirts in the closet, and I won't pay 89 cents for a glass of juice when water is available. Yet I forked out $39.95 for a sweatshirt that was

just a $9.95 shirt with some silly local logo on it.

I heard someone the other day, living under stress of debts, divorce, doubts about the future and extremely frustrated with all she had to handle, telling a group with great humor the only way out of this low was to get some therapy—"retail therapy." That was a new one on me, so I asked for a definition. Well guess what, retail therapy is "going shopping!"

For some reason, people feel good when they shop. The results, however, eventually add to the problems that caused the need for therapy. Is the pleasure of purchasing worth the pain of paying for things, caretaking them, and then disposing of them? …and it will be pain.

Junk control, watching where you are going, saves tons of repair of where you've been.

"Easy come, easy go" is more like "easy come, easy stay."

THINK!
ONE HEAD, TWO FEET

Contingency planning is smart and economical, and duplicates of some things do make sense, for convenience, backup protection, or reasonable rotation. Even triplicates in things like shirts and skirts can be a good idea, but don't fall into the mindless multiplication trap. Something may be "cheaper by the dozen," but that doesn't mean you should stock up to the load limit—keeping means cost and care. Real security is in minimum these days, not maximum. Why use your life up sustaining things you don't use?

EVEN ONE MAY BE TOO MUCH

Often we think "too much" is a matter of multiplication—more than one, or too many of something. But as a young executive from the local atomic energy plant pointed out, "I have too many boats... I have one."

We don't have a right to, or need for, even one of **everything**. "None"

is often a wonderful and sane solution.

Years ago, when we had less, many things might indeed have been "nice to have." But today, with walls and halls, closets and clothes drawers, minds and garages bulging with "too much," maybe we've finally reached the point where it "**wouldn't** be nice to have...."

You may be able to pay for it, but can you afford it?

"CONSIDER THE SOURCE"

When I was in high school, this expression was what you used to put down or discredit any nonsense laid on you. One would consider the source of the statement or the item, equate it with worthless, and pass it off.

A leading advertiser told me that every one of us is bombarded (hundreds of times a day) with offers and suggestions from all kinds of avenues, inviting us to feel, touch, take, buy, smell, weigh, handle, borrow, try, taste, etc. Those messages are all meant to sell us something, get us to let loose of our time and money... and we do. Most of us without hesitating will take and keep a product, a recipe, a view, an idea from someone who absolutely has no qualifications on it or knowledge of what they are endorsing or advertising. The only thing necessary to let them add to our too much is that they be famous.

How subtle these encouragements for too much can be, too. I was watching an Olympic race on TV once, and the announcers were expertly analyzing and projecting as the well-publicized runners rounded the last stretch. As one of the favorite and "predicted winner" athletes pulled away from the pack near the finish line, the announcer rejoiced and excitedly said, "Well, folks, he has one Mercedes in the parking lot now, he can line up another!" How innocently a remark like this indicates the reward for winning or achieving anything of merit—not only having the best, but adding extra. How does one drive two Mercedes?

WATCH OUT FOR THOSE LYING LABELS

"Low fat," "less cholesterol," "lite beer," "limited numbers," tell us nothing because if the subject is that insidious "too much" then lower, less, lighter, limited is still excess, a punisher of your person!

Socially acceptable or popular is not a sanctifier, either. Labels like "the cutting edge," "cool," "mature," "fashionable," or "popular" don't add up to desirable.

Advertisers and copywriters have a whole vocabulary of "button-pushing" words they use to get us to reach for our credit cards or check-books. In the color insert ad from a popular electronics firm, for example, I noticed all of the following "must have" words used in describing the different products and models:

"Great buys"
"Specials"
"Most wanted"
"Get the second one for a penny"
"Fun maker"
"Mini handheld"
"Add to your…"

"Super selection"
"Bonus"
"Everyone needs…"
"Portable"
"Whole system"
"Bargain"
"Upgrade"

Another phrase to be wary of: "As seen on TV." How being on TV amounts to total sanctification for people I'll never know, but it has almost an unquestioned credibility. I will be somewhere mingling with the crowd like any other guest or member of a group, until someone says, "He's been on TV!" People then treat me like a celebrity.

Before your next rush to get a pen and paper in the aftermath of a power ad on the tube, take a hard, objective look at all the rest of what is "on TV." You'll probably come to your senses. Take "on TV" as a warning, not a seal of approval.

FORGET WHAT OTHERS ARE DOING

Quit doing things because others do them, going along with the gang, ordering when and what they order. Select your own sources of consumption and entertainment, question who says it when you hear that something is a "must have," a "must see," or a "must buy"… put up your own detour sign.

DON'T LOOK AND YOU WON'T GET TOOK

"Just browsing"—what good ever came of browsing (unless you're a cow or deer). Think about it—when you spend time checking out and hanging around a neat boutique or new car showroom, you're just plain cruising for a choosing. Browsing is the sire of buying, generally not just what you don't need, but the best of what you don't need.

Between interviews in New York one day, for example, I ran down to the street during lunch to pick up some scotch tape and ruler in the only store nearby. It turned out to be an "odds and ends" shop, and had everything under the sun except tape and rulers. The aisles were so packed that you couldn't move—you had to wait for a surge or a flow in the direction you hoped to go. There were scores of New Yorkers in there in a buying frenzy. Since the merchandise was all over the lot, had no rhyme or reason, it was clear that most of those browsers were there just for something to do to kill time. People were pawing through total trash, squeezing, patting, and stretching things to test some hidden quality they might have. Two well-dressed gentlemen, for example, were checking out a plastic sphere. I had no idea what it was, nor did they. The conversation went like this:

(One fellow, picking the item up) "Wow, look at this, Harry!"

"What is it?"

"I don't know, but it's heavy, feels good."

The other man, now suitably enthused with the find, said (I kid you not), "Well, it's only 88 cents—let's get it!"

Most of us would like to think we'd never be this dumb about acquisition, and maybe we would exercise admirable prudence in the "under a dollar" stores. But once we are immersed in the ambience of a shopping mall or expensive store of any kind, even the tiniest temptation is triggered into a full-scale inclination to shoot the works. We settle on, "Well, it's only $29.95... let's get it."

Am I telling you to resist the temptation of accumulation? Nope. I'm telling you to **avoid** the temptation. None of us are as good at resisting as we imagine we are. You don't have to be an expert at refusing offers if you aren't present when the offer is made.

Knock-knock... "Who's there?"
"No-see-um." "No-see-um who?"
"No see um, no want um!"
Amazing, how many classified ads and catalogs we don't need to read once we savor the pleasures of being clutter-free.

REMEMBER THE DIFFERENCE BETWEEN WANTS AND NEEDS

We've all heard a score of sermons on the difference between wants and needs, but most of us still don't have this quite sorted out yet. By instinct, we want it all, and there are many brilliant financiers and marketers who work day and night to find a way to make it possible for us to obtain it all. Remember the difference between wants and needs, and beware of the creeping move from wants… to needs… to deeds!

THINK!
WHY ARE YOU BUYING THIS?

The following are the boiled-down basic reasons we gain weight in our homes and storage areas. We usually buy something because:
- we want to show it off (flaunt it)
- we intend to use it (do we?)
- we're going to stash it away
- we're "addicted" (couldn't say no)
- "it's an investment" (lots of wishful thinking here)
- we were bored

We accumulate a lot of our clutter just for something to do, we wander around collecting stuff and then looking for a place to store it, or a sentence to explain why we have it. The next time you're tempted to buy something, stop long enough to figure out why you want it.

Don't ever underestimate the combination of idleness, exposure, and convenience as an accelerator of accumulation and "I wonder why I bought this?"

CONSIDER
OBSOLESCENCE

Always consider the obsolescence potential of anything you're considering taking on, or making part of your life. What doesn't last and is no longer loved will always put weight on you in some way.

As a friend pointed out to me wistfully one day, "Ah yes, I just had to have one of those big satellite dishes ($5000 when they first came out!) I feed the cattle hay out of it now."

NEW MAY BE BETTER…
BUT IS IT NECESSARY?

One big source of clutter is always having to have new and better when the old is working fine. Every salesperson's aim is to make us dissatisfied with "the old one." But out of date doesn't mean out of service. My fifteen-year-old Nikon F3 , for example, has more fancy automated features on it than I've figured out how to use in fifteen years. And still it is considered an "old manual," out of date.

Not long ago I dug out my forty-year-old Nikon F2, blew the dust off, loaded it up, put in a new battery, and shot a couple of rolls at a church picnic. The prints were so clear people peered at them in amazement, and it took all of 1/8 of a second to focus each time, by hand. I look around and see camera waste on every side, piles of automated, do-it-all-for-yous, in duplicate, for just one person. And very few pictures coming out.

In my shop, too, I have tools that are just as fast as the newer auto-mated ones, that don't break down, and don't need batteries or electric cords. Many of these are thirty and forty years old and older. Why be in such a rush to "upgrade"? High-tech medical gear and some computer and phone equipment might merit imme-diate update, but don't be too quick to abandon those "old manuals." Many modern machines are so complicated and automatic that after a while we often just don't use them. It's not worth the mental strain, digesting the 110-page booklet that comes with them, and reading and figuring out how to use all the option buttons.

Why are we always want-ing more and better when we aren't using the things we already have?

The urge to own the newest and best, the latest technology, creates a lot of clutter and credit card debt. People constantly ask me how I can get along without a car phone. Though I own and manage companies in several states, and have family, community, and church matters to tend to all over, I haven't found a fully practical use for a car phone yet. If you are prepared and early, when do you need one? And do you really want to be distracted by one while driving? Many of my managers have them, and what I mostly see (while I'm riding with them) is them calling wives on their way home to tell them what time they will be home. This is something they could do from the office more cheaply and courteously. My point here is not against car phones, in some businesses and circumstances they are a real asset. But having them when you don't really need them is another tool to pay for, hunt for, tend, lock up, and be interrupted by. All in all making life harder to live, not easier.

Or consider that famous garage tool so many hobbyists aspire to, the ShopSmith, capable of performing the tasks of a dozen different power tools. Yet ninety percent of these amazing mutants are used mainly as a table saw in the end. Yet they are much more costly than a table saw, and it's harder to isolate a problem when they need fixing.

Computers, likewise, can do an unbelievable number of things, it's true. However many computer owners are at the point of panic over this. They don't want, need, use, or understand all of the extras their machines are packed with. It's said that the average person only uses about 13% of the features and capacities of all of their computer programs and hardware. A few aficionados demand ever more options and bells and whistles, while the average person helps pay for it all but only uses a few. He could probably get along just as well with the "older" version of software and hardware he already has. Another case when new may not be necessary.

> *Use what you have. "Getting by" and "making do" were once not just the standard, but something to be admired.*
>
> *People talk constantly about, getting back to the basics, even as they are gearing up to get more, bigger, better, and faster—behavior that only takes them ever farther from the basics.*

BEWARE OF GADGETS

I've made many in-person appearances at home shows, those garden or home remodeling shows held every spring and fall at huge arenas or convention centers. The aisles are lined with hundreds or even thousands of booths, merchants giving shows and demonstrations on everything imaginable, from hot tubs to salad makers, ginseng to knife sets. On every side is someone showing and selling a magic tool or miracle formula, while thousands of people shuffle by taking it all in.

It never ceases to amaze me that the biggest crowds always seem to be gathered at the booths with the most questionable products. People watch and believe the pitchman, who saw the product for the first time himself three hours ago. Then they clamor to lay down a chunk of cash for a handy-dandy, rinky-dinky thing they'll never use or that won't work

"I press this button &... ba-da-boom ... It's a scooter... in case your car runs outta gas on the expressway...just drive it home."

once they get it home. The glamor and glitter of gadgets pulls people out of good sense into purchase, purchase, purchase, pack home, piddle with it, and then stick it someplace, to crowd the cabinet or rattle around in a drawer. Be warned when your heart starts warming toward some new gadget. Get solid tools, not gadgets.

Don't buy things you can't use

This is a day of owned but not used. I was the major employer in Sun Valley, Idaho, a ski resort town, for six years. In the course of this I did a lot of maintenance and repair work in and around nice homes. Sun Valley had become a place where movie stars and other rich people came and overpaid for property and put on huge homes worth five to fifteen million dollars. The elegance of these homes was a topic of conversation for every tradesman working in them. Many of these homes were built long distance—the owners never showed up during the process, and the builders/workers just received calls and messages from them about things to be done or enacted. Then after the house was finished it sat vacant most of the time, because the owner was too busy and famous to use it much. These edifices were mostly good for magazine articles on them, so that all of us with ordinary little homes could drool over them. This giant and expensive piece of

property was of little value to the owner, just something to plan, to build, to protect, to maintain, and to pay for forever.

We all do this on a smaller scale. We may criticize the big spenders, but a lot of little rash spending equals the same outcome. Don't buy things, large or small, that you can't or won't use.

"I have three fly rods and I haven't fished for five years. Maybe I'll buy another one, and that will compensate for not going fishing as much." (Junker's logic.)

Forget "FREE"

Not long ago at a women's show a 200-foot long line filed past the booth where I was doing vacuum demonstrations. I asked the women in it: "What line is this?" They answered, "I don't know, but whatever they are offering, I want one!"

Once during the taping of a TV program I was to appear on, to get the studio audience warmed up the host yelled "How many of you would like to get some free stuff?" Enthusiastic cheers, shrieks, yells, and "Yeah, man's" ensued, though no one in that audience had a clue as to what was to be given away. But it was FREE. The evaluation of bad or good, needed or not needed, is totally blotted by "free."

In the final stages of planning and designing our low-maintenance home on Kauai, for example, my wife and I decided to go to the annual home and garden show in Honolulu. So we called for information and tickets, for the event itself and the plane trip to it. There was (of course) a "deal" that included a free rental car with the flight. My wife excitedly reported this bonus to me. "But we don't need a car," I told her. "It won't cost us one cent more," she said. "We've got to take it!"

Yes, the car was free, but… I explained the costs to her. "When we arrive in Honolulu, fifty feet from the Aloha Airlines gate, we can catch a nice fast city bus for $1, which will take us right to the front steps of the exhibition center. Then just $1 for the return trip, no stress, and we can sit back and enjoy all the sights on the way. That 'free' car is going to take one hour to check out and check in, insurance and gas will be $15.50, parking at the convention center will take 20 minutes and cost $5, and then finding maps and driving in the congested downtown of an unfamiliar city isn't exactly my idea of a day off." (Now there is some divorce fuel—me driving and my wife trying to navigate our way through all those ten-foot wide, one-way Honolulu streets.) The free car was a wonderful example of how "free" can end up costing us wasted time, money, and emotion. Most free things end up

kicking around the house or cluttering up a storage area somewhere.

> *"My friend got a free car through an ad in the paper. It was a '78 Datsun wagon, had been in a front end collision, and had lots of body rust. It also needed a new radiator, a new alternator, and I don't know what else. I'd love to see how much she spent in insurance, title transfer, and repairs, on this 'free' car (not to mention her time)."*

DON'T TAKE OR USE IT BECAUSE IT'S THERE

Why do we do it? Most of us do, you know. We get a voucher, per diem allowance or budget for food, for example, such as when we're on a business trip or our flight is delayed, and we force ourselves to use it all up. Often we don't need it, we aren't hungry, but it is ours, we have a coupon for it or it's being served, so we strain to use or consume it all. There seems to be some stigma about leaving anything for someone else, or just skipping the "free lunch." I've watched superintelligent and ignorant people alike inflict indigestion and nerve damage on themselves, trying to use all of a voucher, in order to "get their money's worth."

We'll always take samples of food, yardsticks, pens, free newspapers or magazines, stickers, ball caps, or key chains.

It's as if availability were the question, not what is needed or right for us.

> *"I grew up with a mother whose favorite sayings were:*
> *1. 'That's a perfectly good _____' (this was usually said while viewing someone else's trash, and yes, we always snatched up the item in question).*
> *2. 'Stop the car!!!' (to pick up other people's trash, or for any garage sale anywhere).*
> *3. 'Someone could use that' (it usually wasn't us)."*

Forget "my share"

Ever really think about what "your share" means? We tend to think of our share as kind of an equality of ownership—share is seldom evaluated in terms of what will actually benefit us, only as possession of some equal portion of a commodity at hand. A "right" to something doesn't necessarily mean we need, deserve, or have to have it—look how slow we are to claim our share of debt or blame. And how demanding we can be when it comes to a piece of cake, an allotment, inheritance, or handout.

Going for a share just because it is there invests you in "Too Much, Incorporated."

Forget "SALE"

If you want to see motivation for more, even for those with "too much," just remove the "for" from a "for sale" sign. Almost everything is for sale, but used alone "SALE" becomes the most powerful, seductive word in our language. Even the best defenses are breached when there is wind of a real "sale." You can get another of something you have and don't use, cheaper than the first one. (Then we buy it on our credit cards, where the interest often pushes the cost higher than the pre-sale price ever was.) "Wholesale" and "factory outlet" likewise numb our noodles, and price clubs and co-ops have a way of convincing us that because it costs a little less, we have a right—a need—to claim it!

A husband, for example, bought his wife a Sam's Club card and went in to look the store over. He ended up carrying three shopping carts of stuff out. Need wasn't the decision factor,

it was just that the deals were too great, you could get two for one, even if you really didn't need the one. (My wife admits she has twelve pair of "two for one" shoes she hasn't worn once yet.) Another woman of my acquaintance, whose children are all grown now, bought one gallon of hot-dog relish at a warehouse club, because the price was just too low to pass up. That big jug is still jamming her refrigerator, and she's still passing out free jars of relish to everyone she knows.

The word "sale" is bad enough, now just add the word "season" and even the firmest will fold—winter, spring, summer, fall sales give us permission to pile up the place. Those "trouble" sales really make us buy, too, because when others are in a forced situation we just know they are "bottom dollar desperate." Lost our lease sale, out of business sale, clearance sale, fire sale, inventory sale, moving sales will move us to action. Even if we have no money or place to put anything more, we'll be there at 6 a.m. Stick a number in front of sale, too, and watch out! 30%, 40%

or 50% off will mesmerize us into taking in "too much." A famous person's name will work this amazing magic, too—Washington, Lincoln, Columbus, even the Easter bunny linked up with "sale"—means one more chance to get the good deals. Yard sale is a cheap shot, but watch a misspelled, crooked, cardboard sign with this scribbled on it pull in the passerbuyers!

From a letter: "The only difference between a yard sale and a trash pickup is how close to the road the stuff is placed."

THE WORD "SAVE"— A REAL SEDUCER

SAVE, too, is a real seducer and a prime example is long-distance calling. As competition in the industry has increased it's driven prices down, which is one reason for all those sales calls we get from MCI, Sprint, AT&T, and all the rest of the pack, asking us to sign up for their latest system because we will "save so much."

With all of these savings, what sometimes seems like unbelievable savings on the cost of phone calls, are our phone bills lower? No way. Home phone bills, which once were ten or twenty dollars, are now into the hundreds. Why? Because calls are "now so cheap" that we are doubling and tripling our phone use. We think

that with each call we are saving, so the more calls we make, the more we save… that's pretty poor logic, and millions now have stunning long distance and cellular phone costs to prove it. By the end of the month we spent $200 instead of the $50 we would have spent when the prices were so high.

SALE and SAVE are entirely immaterial to something we don't need, something that isn't necessary in our life. Our crew travelled down to El Paso, Texas, once, for example, to give a workshop on cleaning up your place and possessions. We gave our presentation to an enthusiastic crowd, leaving them committed to cut down clutter and cleaning time. I had one last speech to give alone, which left the rest of my crew with some free time to do whatever they wanted. There was not a drop of doubt or delay—in an instant, they were headed across the border to Mexico, only three miles away.

"What are you going to do there?" I asked.

"Buy stuff," was the answer.

"Such as what?" I questioned. (They'd all been complaining about their overloaded homes on the drive down.)

"Well, nothing we can think of right this minute, but…"

"But what??"

"In Mexico things are so cheap, Don! Leather purses, for instance, are only about a quarter of the price they are here in the states."

"But you have at least a dozen good purses now, all over the place."

"You just don't understand, they are so inexpensive…."

True, I just don't understand!

How many of us have extra purses around, and haven't been across a border yet?

FORGET "DEALS"

When you hear some say that a deal was "a steal," you've generally heard a great truth. Most deals steal your time, money, emotion, wits, and space. One woman, who started back in 1960, now has over a thousand cookbooks. She said her entire collection started from a brochure on a cookbook club addressed to "resident," wherein for just one dollar you could get three entire books. She picked the largest, on the assumption that they would tell her the most, and you know the rest now.

A while ago I asked a young couple who were excited about a coming trip to Las Vegas why they were going, as I knew they didn't gamble, weren't drinkers, and not even particularly entertainment oriented. Plus they had a little family and both worked, so they would have to be away from their children and their jobs for a few days. Their reason for going?

"It was so cheap! We got air fare, a rental car, and two nights in a motel for $98."

"All because it is a deal," I noted.

"More than a deal," they said. "Even a bargain trip to Las Vegas normally costs about $400, so we are saving $300, and we just couldn't pass that up."

Amazing. They were willing to spend several days away from home, wandering through a bunch of noise and lights, overeating and wasting time, mainly because it was a bargain.

"Since I dejunked, I've saved all that time I used to spend every day scanning ads and newspapers for deals. Junk-free is the best deal I ever made or got."

"Go" doesn't have to mean "get"

I'll be the first to admit that bringing a gift home from a trip to a spouse, child, or coworker can indeed be a nice little addition to the quality of life. But things aren't like they used to be. Not long ago only a few traveled, and only once in a while. Now most of us are mobile, and some of us do ten or more trips in a single month! Our base of relationships has broadened, too. As time passes our family and circle of friends is bigger, and there are more people who work with, for, and around us. All of which triples if not quadruples the eager expecters when you get back.

For years I worked to keep up the pace of procuring something worth giving to family and friends when I returned. It threatened to become the central focus of my trips. I had to plan my purchases before a trip, and make them on the way there and while there (sometimes missing meetings and the like to do it). Then I had to cushion breakables, find a way to keep perishables cool and to carry awkward things, and protect all the packages on the way home. After all this, much of the time the recipients either already had what I got them or had no place to put it. So a harmless little thing, a good thing, became much and then too much. Now that I limit my travel gifts, I've noticed neither hostility nor longing glances at my suitcases when I return. Instead I see a marked increase in my own productivity in my travels, which ultimately blesses everyone more than any number of trashy trinkets I could lug home.

"Go" doesn't have to mean "get," although we seem to have been taught that somehow. On the cover of a senior citizen's magazine the other day, for example, I noticed a big feature article titled "Going Places." I figured this would be about making trips or excursions that would expand our talents and family ties, hobbies and second professions. Until I read the fine print under the title: "Cruising, food, wine, and bargains..." Going places this way won't do anything to declutter our golden years.

In our effort to "get away from it all," we have the tendency to take it all with us. In tourist or convention towns, the streets are lined with gift shops, the exact sort of thing that most people have travelled to get away from. But here they are now right in the mecca of "too much," and

149

soon they are walking out remove with armloads of stuff they didn't want or need, don't know what to do with or where to put.

A couple I know were traveling on a tour boat through some of the most beautiful land in Alaska. They had five hours of shore leave, and used it all walking the streets, where there were nothing but souvenir shops. The husband finally collapsed perspiring on a bench, and said to his wife wearily, "well, where else?"

A focus on "getting something" in life often takes too much time and attention away from "becoming something" personally. We seem to think of acquiring in terms of hardware, rather than the emotions or uplift we might experience just letting something be absorbed into our being—a feeling, a song, a view, an insight. Instead we seem to opt for a chunk of wood, plastic or metal, or a piece of cloth with a saying on it. Our clutch on "too much" blocks out many of the finer things of life.

NOTHING IS DUTY FREE

Getting ready to board a flight one day, I noticed passengers loaded down with much more than travel luggage—they had stuff sticking out of every conceivable style of bag and bundle. The source of this seemed to be the "duty-free" shop and its enticing array of liquors, tobacco, perfumes, jewelry, and gifts.

That took nerve, calling this stuff "Duty Free." Nothing is duty free. If it adds even an extra ounce of weight, you'll be paying that duty tax in installments for many moons thereafter.

Hold down the holidays

I made a mean decision this February, or did I?

I looked at the upcoming and ever-expanding Valentine season and realized I was in an "all or nothing" valentine-sending situation. I decided on the nothing, and so didn't give one single valentine, not even to my wife, who said, "Hooray, we saved money, clutter, and lots of time better spent."

Don't get me wrong—I've long been a fan of the spirit of the day. In grade school Valentine's Day was the sensation of the year in some boring

"THAT'S WHAT HAPPENS WHEN YOU PACK THE SOUVENIRS TOO TIGHT!"

classes and drab buildings. I loved exchanging valentines with my peers—it was a good growth experience and a chance to make some bold commitments when it came to selecting who would get that single "I love you" valentine, the only one. Valentines were a wonderful experience clear through the eighth grade.

My decision to have a "heartless" February 14th this year was reinforced when my wife and I (though we were 2500 miles apart) both went to a local "mart" and saw several aisles full of Valentine stuff. Even poor, struggling families were buying $30 and $40 worth of red trash, candy they didn't need, pillows, stuffed animals, and other trinkets that would be trashed within hours of receipt by whoever received them. Today, there isn't just one class sweetheart, a mother, plus maybe a favorite aunt to consider—it's a full-blown disease… enough to make you heartsick!

I have at least seventy-five women now whom I love and are worthy of heartfelt thanks or a special little remembrance from time to time. Besides my beloved mother, there are ten granddaughters, four daughters, a couple of aunts, twenty-five women who work right in the office with and around me every day, and twenty more who contribute constantly to my books, media appearances, and general welfare. There are at least forty more at church, from grade-school age girls to seasoned, life-influencing teachers. All of these

people are worthy of a Valentine's Day recognition and I have addresses for all of them. And so a full-fledged following of the Valentine ritual would take me two solid days and cost more than a thousand dollars, in time and money. That doesn't seem right to spend on a day that is just a pleasant custom, after all, not necessarily a remembrance time of my own choosing or when my heart just feels like "doing something."

All year round I nurture, help, worry about, and look after these Valentine-worthy girls and women, sending them books, taking my time to be in touch, and spending money on them. I pay many of them good salaries, and hopefully will continue to do so, forever. But as for today, it had reached the "too much" point, and I had to go for "all or none." So I

picked none, and chose to use the time and money for better purposes.

I did this with Halloween, too, thirty years ago, and also Easter—the commercialized Easter Bunny eventually gnawed away my appreciation for the event. Once you get on the holiday hayride, it will take you for a ride—do the steering, stopping, and loading for you, all at your expense.

Don't be afraid to trim back the holidays to fit your own situation, means, or taste. You'll have less stress, less clutter, and enjoy the days you do celebrate more.

Make your path public

We don't acquire **all** of our excess intentionally—some of it comes in the form of gifts, awards, inheritance, handouts, junk mail, or other "free-bies." We didn't seek it out, but somehow we ended up housing it.

One thing that will help here is to make your standards and policies about junk and clutter clear to every-one… everywhere. Then others (a big source of clutter) will stop giving you, sending you, or even offering you anything of questionable worth. Shed your unwanted stuff publicly and others will get the idea fast. Before you toss some silly or ugly piece of clutter, tell the world that you didn't want it and haven't got space for anything like it. Have no clutter around you, and people will avoid filling your space. As soon as

"they" get the message that you aren't messing around, that managing stuff isn't your favorite pastime, they will lay off laying it on you.

You'll know you've clipped this umbilical cord of attainment when people start complaining, "Boy, are you hard to buy for." What a compliment it is when people are afraid to give you anything that might fall under the category of "junk." You'll have less unsolicited clutter, and the quality of the gifts you do get will improve dramatically.

Look at your lifestyle

Some time, preferably today, stop and look at your lifestyle. Maybe it is your way of living that is causing the result you aren't pleased with. Long-established habits such as shopping for entertainment, fad following, hobby hopping, or "overkill" of any kind may be encouraging that frightening flow of clutter to your car and your closets.

Live lean

My father was a master manager, and the older I get, the more I search back into the many years we worked together in my youth for the ways he managed to be so productive in his life, for the benefit of not only our whole ranching operation but every one of us in the family.

One virtue I didn't see then, but recognize now, was his habit of living lean. We lived well, better than kings, but lean. Nothing ever seemed crowded, excessive, overdone. At Fourth of July picnics, or Thanksgiving or Christmas feasts where more and better food than we can comprehend now was available, Dad always ate one plateful. Leaving the table lean, or a little hungry, rather than "overstuffed," always gave you an edge for staying healthy and active. People who "live it up" are usually rewarded by having to live it down. His theory was "live lighter, live better," an opposite philosophy from ninety-five percent of marketing and merchandising.

Don't be afraid to "go without"

Fortunately I come from people who had the foresight to record their life in journals, that generations later were collected into a "family history" book. Not only is it fascinating to read about my forebears boating from Europe, establishing colonies in the New World, and crossing the plains, but to see what and how well they endured, battling snowstorms and droughts, Indians, wild animals, hunger, injury, illness, and sudden violent death. Hardships only seemed to strengthen their family closeness and ideals. Loyalty, love, and simple things provided a savor we seem to be searching for earnestly now, but cannot find.

These histories offer clear evidence that a crisp, rewarding life can indeed be lived without a sports car, fancy clothes, lavish jewelry, big houses and yards, portfolios of investments, and perks of all kinds.

If you talk to the people today who had to "go without" once, or early in life, most of their comments on this are positive. People see it as a good and valuable experience, a time of closeness and building and learning. Even those who have experienced some real struggles say that living with less and going without was the best time of their lives, in retrospect. They did more, felt more, and developed personally more—it was a time of real closeness to family and nature. Then we get well heeled enough to go anyplace or do or own about anything for ourselves and our families and life begins to close in on us.

I noticed this month, paging through the beautifully printed pages of one of our great homekeeping publications, that there was almost nothing on good homekeeping. It was— articles and ads alike— almost all about exotic, expensive food and clothes, movie stars, glamour, and cosmetics. There was very little on how to manage and live better at home, only how to get and own every new, automated, overdesigned this and that.

Coping with those cluttered choices

Our grandparents and great-grandparents really had limited choices and opportunities. There were only a few things available to eat, wear, own, travel in, watch, read, or entertain yourself or others with. So considering the alternatives and making choices and judgments was relatively simple. Sometimes they didn't even have any choice!

Our parents had a new world of more products, machines, and services than ever before, and much more widespread ways of making the availability of all this known to them. And look at you and me and everyone, today—as noted earlier, we have a endless galaxy of opportunities. We have much more money, greater access to everything, unlimited internets of information, and no end of products and brands to buy and places to go. With the aid of extended payment plans and credit cards, we can own or have almost anything we want, do anything we want, go anywhere we please. All of us, even the poorest of us, have more to choose from than kings did a hundred years ago. So understandably we are getting bogged down if not stuck in the consideration and selection process.

Our Great-Grandparents' day...

Today...

There is so much, even in the average store, we actually have to stop our life to consider the options before we can proceed with whatever we're about. We could easily spend a month of our lives reading labels in the cereal aisle of the supermarket alone, for example.

We can't say all the opportunities available these days are "bad" because they aren't. Many of them are blessings, but the limiting factor here is that we can't want and have it all (Lord knows we're trying)—we haven't the room to retain it. Just think for a minute of how much you have on hold or under consideration, how much you want, are waiting for, or fully or halfheartedly pursuing. It might be magnificent stuff, but it can easily become malignant.

What is the answer? Direction!

There is a big benefit in doing "media" (appearing on TV and radio and in newspapers) besides the publicity. Those reporters, hosts, and commentators are always pushing and hounding you for a short, succinct, "bottom line" answer to the problems at hand. Such as "Why do people become junkers, Don?"

Over the years, from thousands of voluntary contributors and confessed clutterers, I've built up quite a list of "why." Like "It was a gift," sentiment, vanity, "I was raised in the Depression," "I'm a Dane," heredity, the environment, insecurity, etc. There are pages of reasons. When I squeeze these people like the media squeeze me for a one-word or one-sentence summary, it generally boils down to... indecision. I just can't decide what, when, and where, so I take and get everything that is there.

That's the bottom line, and now what is the cause of that indecision? Here lies what I believe is the real core of life's clutter—LACK OF DIRECTION! I think it is that simple. When you know where you are going, you know what to carry. I find

that most of the overloaded can't tell you what they really want in life. Direction is somewhat of a mystery to them. I'm meeting more people than ever these days who give me a blank look when I ask "What are your life goals, where are you going, what are you doing this for?" They don't know, so they build an arsenal to cushion themselves and provide for every possibility. Notice that people who really know what they are doing and why—their life purpose—seem to carry a minimum of extras. If you know where you are going you'll know if you need something or not. People who are a little confused about what they want and where they are headed, take it all, as much as they can carry, just in case... (they might need it someday).

You need direction before you can direct the "too much" traffic in your life. Needs are easy to see and decisions almost make themselves, when a clear direction is established. I'm convinced all of us have the strength and smarts for the "what" and "how" to get rid of, once we see of what we really need, to get where we want to go. Once you map out your intended journey, you know what to pack.

So sit down some bright morning or quiet afternoon and spend one of the most important hours of your life—deciding, determining, or simply articulating your goals. Write out what you really want to do in the next year, decade, or the rest of your life. Staying junk-free will be much easier afterward.

Now what about....

~~The~~ Our Environmental "TOO MUCH"?

Over the past thirty years, we've received millions of pieces of mail, and listened to and read the warnings of all kinds of experts, advising that the earth's ecological system (balance) is being threatened from all directions. With what? We already know the answer—TOO MUCH!

Being much interested myself in the preservation of the planet, I dug through all my files to isolate what the environmental issues actually are, and I found not one or two, but nine!

- ***Air pollution and global warming (the air we need to breathe and the ozone layer we need to protect us)***

- ***Water pollution (which affects the water we drink, and like to play in)***

- ***Litter and clutter***

- ***Household waste***

- ***Hazardous waste***

- ***Deforestation and loss of wetlands (loss of habitat for wild animals and birds)***

- ***Land erosion (loss of the topsoil we need to grow our food)***

- ***Mineral/Oil depletion***

- ***Damage to our state and national parks***

True, we do have to live. However if you review this list thoughtfully, I think you'll see that the overload here is not from what we need or use to live, but from "too much." We (ourselves and our country as a whole) could cut all of these down as much as 50 percent if we only controlled how we eat, what we use, what we waste, and how we treat things.

We are approaching this problem like we do other problems—we continue to heap it on and then after awhile we complain and go for the girdle cure. And so our solution here is to make laws and regulations that only organize and regulate the "too much," rarely reduce it.

These trips to the dump take <u>way</u> too much time since it moved up north.

For years now, for example, panic-stricken "do-gooders" have been telling us that before long we are going to bury ourselves in our own trash. They are right, we are! Like most of you, I grew up counting on the city, the county, or a commercial garbage hauler they hire to pick up all those "leftovers" and dispose of them, make them disappear. And the taxes, charges, and fees for this weren't too bad. Now those fees are going up and we read and hear everywhere about how there is too much waste and trash, and not enough room for it. Barges are circling our harbors, searching for a new dumping place. And it's not just "New York's problem." I live in Idaho where we have more than forty acres per person. But I'm also in the profession of cleaning buildings and handling the fallout from them, and I too see what is happening. There is indeed too much, too much trash and we (if not you and me, then our grandchildren or great-grandchildren and their loved ones), are going to be buried by it.

The fact that we ignore this will never make it go away.

"TOO MUCH" is an action demand, and that action needs to be self, not communally, initiated.

The earth's obesity problem isn't a social one as we are told, it is an individual problem—government, cities, counties, or clubs can't control it. In fact many of these programs only add to the "too much," while trying to "unmuch" it.

Consider the "Adopt a Highway" program. The more we do-gooders police up those beer and pop cans, the more litter there is. People are tossing more than ever, and we are cleaning up behind them, only reinforcing bad environmental behavior. The junk and

157

clutter is still there, we are just wasting good gas and risking young lives policing it. It is self-policing, not policing, that will save the earth. I may never manage to distribute my extra food to a foreign country, but I can avoid waste, luxury, and excess that will ultimately affect the welfare of the entire world. If enough of us did this, it would make a big difference.

To keep the weight off Mother Nature we all need to live providently:

1. Eat less
2. Buy less
3. Waste less
4. Use, not abuse facilities
5. Clean up our own mess
7. Travel less and stay home more
8. Uncycle (stop adding things to the system), before worrying about recycling
9. Stop smoking (not just ourselves, but our cars and our buildings)
10. De-glamorize (ourselves, our homes, our vehicles, and our habits)

This will do more than all the marches, donations, legislation, campaigns, and pledges.

Embrace a new word, "minimalism," to balance out capitalism and materialism.

But what about Overpopulation?

We hear the question often today: "What is going to happen if the world's population doubles in the next forty years?"

Of course we should be mindful of the possibility of "overpopulation." But the room for we humans is greatly affected by the room taken by, and energy used to produce and run, **things**. The living should of course be our first concern. The world isn't overpopulated, it is underorganized and overjunked. If the time, money, and effort used to pollute and desensitize the world were used to love, care for, and serve humanity, "overpopulation" wouldn't be as much of an issue. The problem of hunger, for example, has more to do with politics and greed, than the amount of room available on the planet. Unemployment, civil unrest, and environmental destruction aren't "human" problems, they again are rooted in our infatuation with material goods. Limiting our constant quest for "too much" would greatly change our view of "too many" as one problem of our planet.

If we all gathered up even one-half of our "overkill" (the objects, clothing, resources, food we don't really need) a lot of those poor families would be well provided for. Try cutting clutter before cutting kids.

The Ten Commandments of KEEPING FREE

1. Honor all good habits that cost and clutter less.

2. Thou shalt not "shop." Just purchase necessities, don't shop.

3. Make thy path public—announce your weightless state so people won't fill your mind, mouth, or living room shelves with "stuff."

4. Thou shalt not commit credit card escalation, testing limits.

5. Thou shalt not covet "sale" merchandise.

6. Ban "junk bunkers" (furnishings, accessories, or structures that do nothing but hold and encourage junk).

7. Do not honor gray areas. It is either Yes you need it, or No you don't. Thou shalt not say Maybe, permitting questionable objects to occupy middle ground.

8. Thou shalt not get the shakes when you have extra room, space, or savings.

9. Hang around with the trim and uncluttered, and you won't have hangups, hangouts, or hangovers.

10. Thou shalt reflect daily on how much more efficient, better off, and better liked you are when you're CLUTTER FREE.

CHAPTER 7

Too Wonderful for Words!

A doctor, who had been a young Air Force commander in World War II, gave me an example of unloading I never forgot. He said "Getting off the ground in England with the tons and tons of bombs in a bomber was almost touch and go. The plane struggled to gain altitude, and it flew heavy. As soon as we crossed over into enemy territory, the antiaircraft fire and flack were intense. We had all that explosive on board, and bullets and shells were hitting and exploding all around us and often zipping through the fuselage and cockpit. But we had to wait until we reached the target area before we could release our deadly cargo.

When the bomb bay doors finally opened and the bombs dropped in plummeting clusters to the munitions factories below, the crew breathed a collective sigh of relief. And the plane lunged upward like a roller coaster, almost uncontrollably, with all that weight gone! No matter how prepared we were for this de-weighting, it was always an amazing sensation."

I lived that intense and unforgettable experience with him as he described it, and thought of how in my own life, when I finally release problems, how my energy and spirit lunges and soars upward, too… being lighter is its own reward.

On a large network radio show, I once asked people to call in and confess the biggest pieces of clutter they had around and needed to, but just hadn't managed to get rid of. We offered a prize for the worst junk and there were some lulus. The winner was a woman who had a school bus in the backyard— old and rusty, wheels and motor gone, but blocked up and used for storage.

About a year later, she called in during another call-in show to tell me she finally had it hauled away. I asked her what kind of reward she got, from the neighbors or otherwise, and she made a classic statement. "No other reward was necessary— when it was gone, I had my view back." That's a pretty profound reward for dejunking, or losing 200 pounds, in this case 20,000 pounds in one day!

As you declutter, you, like the young flyers, will be so surprised. It will be so much better than you anticipated. Letting that two hundred pounds go this weekend will be more like losing a ton or 2,000 pounds, as you discover an unheralded truth of life: less is more, and it brings with it the beauty words like… trim, lean, in proportion, free, peaceful.

There are two hundred rewards for removal of the "too much." Let me just remind you of the big three…

You'll have more room

In your rooms, your closets, your drawers, your agenda, and your imagination. ROOM is a wonderful reward—room to breathe, to think, to put out and place nicely the precious things you've been saving "until later." Room means less stumbling over things and hunting through them, and less explaining, to yourself and others, about the crowded condition of your life.

You'll have more time (for the things you really care about). When you get rid of the garbage, you can do more of the good things.

You'll feel better, and be treated better… by everyone!

Real-life testimonies from born-again nonjunkers:

"I can't believe how flexible and free I feel without clutter!"

"I now go places and enjoy instead of buying stuff with my time."

"Success, oh sweet success. It took me just fifteen minutes to clear the entire room for the tile man. Before dejunking my life, it would have taken me one solid week. Ah, the junkless life, I love it!"

"I love my clean and spacious house now. I love knowing where things are! I LOVE NOT BEING A JOKE AND A MESS!"

"Psychologically, I am someone else now. I have time to go outside with my kids and to play on the floor with them."

"How do I feel now that I've decluttered? How have I most benefitted from the process? I've lost weight, dumped fears, discarded illusions, chucked insecurities, obtained confidences, secured a brighter future, increased my productivity, improved the quality of my life, and sent the 'bigger, better, and more is better yet' philosophy packing."

"There is just something eloquent about being uncluttered."

"The biggest benefit I got from dejunking is that now I know what I have and don't have, and exactly where everything is. Three months ago I could never find a pair of scissors when I needed them."

"I can't believe the time, space, and energy available when you dejunk—things almost self-heal. I can't believe what a relief it is. I used to get depressed and feel like running away. Now I'm sure I don't need to run away—I just need to get rid of some of the things that are cluttering my life. What a great feeling."

"The biggest surprise is not so much the freedom I feel from dejunking, but the horror I feel when I walk into others' homes and see how shackled they are by their junk. It makes me want to shake them and make them realize what their junk is doing to them."

"Thanks again for being one of the biggest influences in my whole life!! I know you have helped so many people who, like me, had kept wondering how to manage all this stuff. Your wonderful answer, at least it worked for me, was: GET RID OF IT!"

"God bless you for your work in throwing us clutterholics a lifeline."

"You have changed my life!"

(No, Mary, you changed your own.)

Not convinced yet?

Listen to this account from Ellen Caplin of what happened when she tossed the clutter in her life.

"After I decluttered:
  1. I started saving money.
  2. With the money saved, I bought a beautiful piano and took piano lessons. I had the time because I no longer was constantly shopping for stuff.
  3. I took a very large and not-my-style ring that I wore MAYBE ten times since my grandmother gave it to me when I was sixteen (twenty-two years ago) and traded it for a lovely emerald ring that I wear every day.
  4. I told my friends not to buy

me whatnot gifts (some listened, some didn't).

5. I invited a friend who reads voraciously to come over to my house and take as many books from my shelves as he wanted. I just kept the ones I REALLY thought I'd read for the first or second time.

6. I took the ones that even he didn't want to the library for their book sale fundraiser.

7. I trashed broken clocks, glasses, dishes, televisions, lampshades, record players, lots of boxes I stored stuff in, old appliances, etc.

8. I continued to save money.**"**

Or how about this "reward report" from an enthusiastic twenty-four year old:

"I have a lot less to clean. I can see all the way under my bed. I can walk freely through my room without following a path. I feel like a much happier person to be around because I have a lot less on my mind. I don't worry about whether or not I lock my door.

You've even affected my eating habits. I have a lot less physical, emotional, and mental baggage now. My friends can sense the difference in me. I've started cleaning up my habits of cursing and eating junk food. I have more self-esteem and a better self-image. I suffer from a mood disorder that I will always need to take medication for, but you've relieved me of a bunch of additional stress and pressure. You've done more for me in three weeks of reading your books than counselors have done in ten years of weekly therapy. I told my psychiatrist to read your books on clutter. Funny how mental health professionals can overlook such a common, deeply affecting problem.**"**

THE LAST EXCUSE ELIMINATED!

And now the last excuse for not decluttering defused. Guess what, folks, of all of the comments people make after their 200-pound week-ends, which of the following would you guess is the most common?

1. "I'm free at last!" Nope.
2. "Wow, I have more room now." Nope.
3. "Gads! I made a heap of money on that old saved stuff." Nope!
4. "I can't believe I didn't do this sooner!" Nope.
5. "I've totally quit mall cruising and going to garage sales." Nope.
6. "My cars are all parked inside for the first time in twenty years!" Nope.
7. "My family and friends all admire me now." Nope.

All of the above are in fact frequent testimonies, but the single most common remark is, "I CAN'T BELIEVE IT DON, I HAVEN'T MISSED ANY OF IT!" Now there is the best reason not to procrastinate our escape from the excess that is now ripping us off. Great, huh?

The big bonus of the 200-pound weekend

The excess that is weighing us down, as we well know, is more than old shoes, broken lampshades, and boxes of heavy magazines. These are the tangible "too muches." The real toughies to toss are the harmful habits and addictions. We know what these are—we could all make a long list of the nasty little things we do, readily admitting that they are harmful to our health, our friends, and our conscience. But suddenly being told, "Don't get mad anymore!" "Quit coming late!" "Stop eating all that chocolate!" "Drive safely!" "Don't swear!" is never going to provide enough power, commitment, or discipline to enable us to just right out quit and reform. These intangible excesses (much to our frustration) have a way of really hanging on, until we outgrow or outlive them. Many people, sad to say, never savor the freedom of conquering them.

Here is the bonus of losing 200 pounds this weekend, and many more in the following weekends. Removing

tangible stuff, junk and clutter, is ten times easier than shedding those emotional intangibles. So first do what you have to do to rid yourself of all the old treasures that have turned to trash. Read *Clutter's Last Stand* or *Not for Packrats Only* (or read them again, if you've already read them), if you want any more information about the principles and procedures involved. And here is my promise: as those tangible items go out of your life, and finally leave some room, a quiet confidence will seep into your soul and testify to you that you don't need "stuff" to be happy.

When you are rid of all that weight you used to deal with daily around your place, you will at last have the self-esteem you've been seeking for so long, in so many ways. Plus a stream of other related virtues like efficiency, strength, endurance, and a sense of confidence and security. And the best part, with the shedding of this stuff, the clutter, there will be an automatic, unsolicited shedding of mental weights like depression and grudges, and the aura of lean will even influence the old diet department. It all flows together, and is a surefire formula for finding freedom from any weight. The biggest reward of all here is the carryover, the pattern you've established—a formula for further personal growth, freedom, and happiness,

The real bottom line of dejunking

But what is the real bottom line of dejunking, cleaning up your life, and being and taking charge of what and who you are, gaining freedom from your burdens? Now you have the capacity to serve others. That is what you are doing all this for, so you are squared away enough that you can help and take care of those in need. Service is the only way man or woman is ever satisfied. Having won't do it, or eating, sports, sex, or travel. These bring a little rush to our lives, but never the blessing we need to be truly happy.

What service am I referring to? Well that is another book and another story, and the answer is deep inside you. You already know what and why to give of yourself. And I promise that the minute you aren't fighting your own battles of what is in, on, and around you, you will have a clearer vision of the needs of others, plus the time, energy, and desire to help. That spirit was built in you when you were born!

As the commercial says, "life doesn't get any better than this!"

One reformed junkaholic made a great comment: "I love people and this earth and I want to make a difference." This is the greatest of all rewards available to us as human beings, to help others and feel you made a difference in some lives, the more the merrier!

A personal code that works for me

Here is a personal code that has really worked for me, to help prevent all those pounds from creeping back on. I call it "Living Providently"—the big 10.

1. Keep yourself, and your place, space, and possessions clean and orderly—uncluttered—no excess.

2. Keep yourself in top physical and emotional condition.

3. Spend less—in accord with your financial capacity and need, not the neighbors or what the networks have to offer.

4. Think of your vehicle as safe, economical transportation—not a matter of ego or status.

5. Work hard—be eagerly engaged in a good cause.

6. Stay home more. Don't waste your real estate. Make home your life center, not the malls, shops, cafes, and stadiums.

7. Take real advantage of what you have, before expanding or getting more.

8. Know the difference between a standard of living and a standard of luxury.

9. Create minimum waste—to help save your personal and our public environment.

10. Take care of those in need, ease others' burdens when you can (save souls instead of stuff, you might say).

Afterword:
200-Pound
Weekend Reports

There is nothing like success reports to make the rest of us want to be more successful. After I finished this book, with I hope enough convincers and arguments to convince you to start your "stuff diet," I still had some great quotes and notes left from the hundreds of reports sent to me every year by readers. I've included them here because I think you might enjoy them or be inspired by them. (See p. 181 if you'd rather send me your own.)

"I couldn't stand to live in a house full of junk any longer. I ended up hauling 12 forty-gallon trash bags of clothes to the Salvation Army, plus several boxes of books and at least four boxes of miscellaneous stuff. I threw out five bags of trash and gave about a quarter of my furniture to some college kids."

"Over the last ten years, I've unloaded:
- many, many shopping bags full of books (I stopped trying to be the local library)
- a closet and bureau full of clothes that just didn't fit me or my life
- several coffee cans full of costume jewelry with the above problem.
- several large boxes of baby clothes I would never put on my child
- several boxes of toys that were redundant or uninteresting to my child (or annoying to me)
- half of the postcard collection I started when I was eight years old
- 2/3 of the vitally important mementos that I was saving—but couldn't imagine why when I went through the box
- two photocopy paper boxes full of neat little things to collage—a hobby I gave up years ago
- 9 boxes of photography equipment
- an ugly wing chair that was uncomfortable as well
- hundreds of record albums, almost 50 cassette tapes, and 15 CDs I am unlikely to ever play again

- the stereo turntable and record cleaning supplies
- hundreds of second-rate photographs and wrecked negatives
- a drawer full of important files, that upon inspection, weren't important at all
- seven really ugly framed pictures my mother didn't want in her house, either
- eight shopping bags full of kitchen items that I never or rarely used
- too many boxes of old, dried up art supplies
- several portfolios of artwork that I had already made portfolio slides of
- all of the extra just-in-case slide copies
- most of my I-might-need-them used cardboard boxes and mailing envelopes.
- ugly seasonal decorations I was never very fond of to begin with.**

**My husband finally decided to do some dejunking over the past few months. He insisted that we have a garage sale, and we did. We made quite a bit of money and took the leftovers (two compact carloads, packed almost to the ceiling) to Goodwill. The tax writeoff this provides looks especially good, since I just sold my business. Here are some of the highlights of our sale:

- He got rid of his Ronald Reagan brown suits. Remember this is 1998, not 1992.
- The floor jacks went. He bought them in 1978 to jack up his former residence, but soon decided the project looked too much like work. Three of the jacks had never been out of the box. He sold them for what he paid for them.
- The punch bowl with 24 cups was bought by a woman who said she put on a lot of baby showers. My husband inherited it seven years ago and it's been stored ever since (obviously, we don't entertain much).
- The box of extra Christmas decorations was the first to go. We held the sale before Halloween.
- Although we still have enough towels for a family of six (and there are only two of us), he did decide to get rid of some that clashed with our bathrooms.
- We took a 1920's chandelier to the local museum, which was glad to get it. I donated it in my husband's honor, which pleased him no end.
- The museum also got some old bottles, toys, and campaign material from past

elections, all in good condition. They were pleased and I was glad to get these things out of our hair.

The living room is now clean, the den looks better, and we can now walk around in the storage unit."

"I just got through rereading *Clutter Free!* and I must admit I learn something new every time I read it. Here is what has happened over the past week or so:

1. We dejunked the bedroom. In the clutter, I found a case of shotgun shells my husband had been looking for (and had gone out and replaced, since he had no idea where they were).

2. My husband agreed to get rid of 3 extraneous pieces of furniture in there.

3. I got rid of 2 extra pillows that we got for our wedding seven years ago.

4. I cleaned out the bookcase, putting a box of books aside for the "do it yourself rummage sale" the YWCA is hosting next month. We've already reserved two six-foot booth spaces.

5. I made a promise to myself not to buy any more books till I'd read the pile of books I'd bought and never touched. I put 80 percent of those books in the rummage sale box after I examined them again.

6. I donated other books to the Friends of the Library book sale that is being held the same day as the rummage sale. That's one way to keep me from buying junk books I don't need.

7. I'm seriously considering giving a racing scrapbook that I've compiled over the past twenty years or so to the historical museum. My priorities have changed. At one time, I was attending over eighty race dates a year at three or four speedways, plus big races, like the Indy 500. Although racing is still my passion, I've attended only about a dozen local events since we got married.

8. I dumped a number of religious tracts that we had been given over the years. We are happy with where we go to church.

9. I cleaned out the refrigerator and threw away (among other things) a jar of Lite mayonnaise that neither of us liked. The pantry is next.

10. We cut our eating out by about two thirds, and now I cook at home. It actually saves time, is cheaper, and I don't mind cooking for my husband and me.

11. My mother recently gave me two T-shirts that she got as souvenirs on a cruise to the Panama Canal. I immediately went through the drawer and put 5 shirts I no longer wear into the sale box.

12. Instead of a birthday present that would create junk in her house, we took Mother out to dinner. Last Christmas I bought her the shoes she needed and sunglasses to replace the ones she lost.

13. A "friend" who is getting on our nerves called the other day—he calls only when he wants something and is an incurable packrat. His house is so cluttered we dread going there. After reading the "Junk on the Hoof" chapter in *Clutter's Last Stand*, my husband and I decided to terminate the relationship.

14. Yesterday, another person called and asked me to be on the board of directors of an organization. I told her I would think about it and call her back. My husband and I discussed it and I told him that although the organization represents a good cause, I was not really deeply committed to it. I called the woman back the next morning and told her, truthfully, that I had a lot

Now THAT'S a load off my mind, Doc.

going on. She said she appreciated my honesty and wished more people would be like that. Afterward, I felt relieved. Before, I would have said 'yes' and then resented every moment of the time I spent on it. **"**

"Aloha Don!

At the end of *Not for Packrats Only* you ask readers some questions about their dejunking.

Here are my answers:

How much junk did you have?

Thirty years worth of accumulated stress from my parents bickering because I was an 'accident.' Thirty years of conditioning from my parents, teachers, peers and others even more misguided than me! Thirty years of bad habits, overdue, uncompleted items, and lack of direction from being muddled and confounded by junk which was both mental and physical.

How long did it take you to dejunk?

In six months I changed my life.

Did you do it all at once or in installments?

In installments. I found that I had to do one thing at a time then go through a small withdrawal. This was followed by research, thinking, and deciding on a better replacement habit or way of life. I then had to inculcate this into my daily activities until it became natural. Once this happened, I was able to see the other areas of my life that needed dejunking. Then I did the next part.

What was the hardest thing about it, the worst problem areas?

Recognizing that to be truly happy and totally myself I would have to make some drastic internal changes. Once this ball got rolling, it quickly put the physical junk in perspective.

Having great friends helps, too, who all read my copy of *Clutter's Last Stand!*

Was any part easier than expected?

Yes, charity.

Many of the things I had to dejunk were brand new and quite expensive but they were of no use to me and therefore had no value. Actually, they had a negative value because I had to care for them!

The joy I got from giving things to others obliterated any loss I might have felt if I just threw things away. Actually, I did not finish as fast as

I could have because I kept looking for more people to give things to!

How did you manage to do it?

Simple. I read your books until the need to dejunk was so overpowering I could not help myself!

It was obvious that my life was filled with junk: things, friends, acquaintances, relatives, habits, places, and a lifestyle that I did not like or want. I decided that I wanted my life to be the way it is in my daydreams, so I changed it!

What was the biggest surprise to you?

The fact that one nanosecond was all it took to make the decision to change my life for the better. Once I made that decision, everything snowballed from there.

Did you find anything that worked especially well to help you to dejunk?

Yes, I noticed that there is a direct relation between stored insecurities and indecision of the mind, stored fat on your body and the stored stuff on your shelves!

By dejunking my physical stuff I lost 12 pounds of excess body weight (so far), several chins and pant sizes.

It feels good to be free!

I was also helped greatly by the realization that we are often so focussed on what we want, that we do not look at what WE have put in our way to prevent us from getting there. If we clear away the obstacles that we have ourselves put in our path, it is much easier then to deal with those imposed on us by others.

I also learned balance. I found that there are empty spaces inside all of us that can only be filled by different things: God, a satisfying career, food, sex, friends, a happy hobby, physical activity, family, growth and development, material things and conveniences, love and romance, and so on. (Not necessarily in that order.)

Often we try to meet these separate needs with just one of the things, e.g., junk material things or other 'crutches.' This leads us to be unbalanced and we usually fall (over our junk!).

Everything is related and when we bring one area into balance we can clearly see the imbalance in others. With our new-found confidence we can then dejunk that area too!

How do you feel you have benefited most from the process?

For the first time ever, I feel light and free to be me. I'm enjoying it!

Would you mind being quoted?

Not at all. I am happy to know that I may help others achieve the freedom and happiness that comes from being dejunked!"

"Dear Mr. Aslett:

I discovered *Clutter's Last Stand* and *Clutter Free! Finally and Forever* about a month ago, and have been fervently decluttering ever since. My husband, son, and I have put eight 30-gallon trash cans out for pickup for each of the past three weeks. (We also generously tipped our trash guys.) But that's not all. We dropped off a dozen vanloads of furniture and clothes at the local charity thrift store, donated hundreds of books to the local library, took a huge bag of knitting supplies to my church (volunteers knit hats and mittens for kids who need them), sold the van (previously considered 'too good' to sell, but not reliable enough to

drive 40,000 miles a year) and our chest freezer.

My five-year-old son even caught the bug; he went through his toys and chose which he wanted to give away and which he wanted to consign at the 'gently used' toy store to raise money to supplement the chore money he's saving to buy a new Lego set.

Finding your books right now, as the new century approaches, was a gift. Being open to change, to empty space, to new ideas, and to God, is so much more fun now that I'm not hiding behind a bunker of junk—paranoid friends, stockpiled food, closets full of clothes, and stuff I was afraid I'd 'need' if I dared to part with it. Getting rid of all this junk in the final months of 1999 is our small act of faith.

I can't say enough good things about you to my friends and family. (Many of them are getting your books for Christmas.) You're the best, Mr. Aslett. THANK YOU. THANK YOU. THANK YOU."

Your 200-pound Weekend Report

Weren't those great, and the greatest thing is that within a few years, I'll have many more even better ones, meaning thousands of more people will be out of the "Pile Prison."

If you would like to share your own "story," the world and I would love to hear from you (Don Aslett, PO Box 700, Pocatello ID 83204). One of your sayings might be the one that saves someone's life… from stuff.

About the Author

DON ASLETT, "America's #1 Cleaning Expert," has been a professional cleaner for over forty years. He has written more than thirty books, many of them bestsellers, including *Clutter's Last Stand, Not for Packrats Only, Clutter Free! Finally and Forever, How to Have a 48-Hour Day*, and perhaps his best known, *Is There Life After Housework?*

Don is the founder and guru of the "dejunking" movement, and this is now his fifth book on the subject, one of the most pressing problems of the modern world. He is 110% convinced that much of what we find unsatisfactory and unsettling in our lives can be removed by a simple three-word program: "DEJUNK YOUR LIFE." This book, and all of his others, is meant to persuade and help readers to do just that.

Don (who still thinks working 14 hours a day is pure enjoyment) is the Chairman of the Board of a 30-state Total Facility Services (cleaning and maintenance) company, a noted and popular speaker, and appears regularly on radio and TV. He has a large family of now grown children, and is active in community and church affairs. He and his wife, Barbara, divide their time between their ranch in southern Idaho and a winter home (a model low-maintenance house!) in Kauai Hawaii.

Thank you

for reading this book. On the next page I've listed a half-dozen of my favorite "clean up your life" books, and page 179 will tell you where you can get them easily and economically. If you want more of these for friends or business associates or groups they are available at quantity discounts. Feel free to write or call and inquire.

Good cleaning, good ~~luck~~ chuck with your dejunking, and *aloha nui*.

Don Aslett

More help with your pursuit of success with excess...

A six-pack of Don Aslett's "FREEDOM BOOKS"— full-length volumes, with all the details.

CLUTTER'S LAST STAND

"The" classic decluttering book, the "dejunker's bible," covering all aspects of junk and clutter. A strong convincer to do something about the "excess" in your life, all of it. Humorous, illustration-packed, thoroughly inspirational! Published by Writer's Digest Books, paperback, 288 pp., $12.99.

NOT FOR PACKRATS ONLY

Gets down to the "what" and "how," the hands-on dealing with all of your clutter caches, and others', too. Plus good solid advice on preventing re-cluttering. Amply illustrated and fun to read. Paperback, 224 pp., $11.95 Published by Marsh Creek Press.

CLUTTER FREE! FINALLY & FOREVER

Here are the confessions and solutions of hundreds of fellow "rats" who have called, written, and bared their souls and storage sheds to Don. How and why they succeeded in clearing their lives of clutter. You'll laugh, cry, and find some real "fuel for flinging" in this one. Published by Marsh Creek Press, 224 pp., $12.99.

THE OFFICE CLUTTER CURE

We all have offices now, often more than one, and they are all buried in papers, periodicals, electronics, tools, trinkets, and cords. Here is help for unburying the office, complete with great visuals. Published by Marsh Creek Press, paperback, 192 pp., $9.99.

KEEPING WORK SIMPLE

A lively, easy-to-read little guide to making office work simpler and saner. 500 tips, rules, and tools to help you do it, including how to clear out the clutter that makes everything in an office harder to deal with, and wastes precious minutes and hours of every day at the office. Paperback, 160 pp., $9.95. Published by Storey Communications.

LOSE 200 LBS. THIS WEEKEND

Decluttering will help not just with the fact that we have too much, but the fact that we are too busy. There is a clear link between too much clutter and too much to do, and reducing the one will automatically reduce the other. This theme will be appealing to the many people who feel the need of "more time" today. Lack of time, stress, and lack of space are three of our biggest complaints today, and all of these will be immediately relieved by decluttering. Paperback, 192 pp., $12.99. Published by Marsh Creek Press.

Other Aslett books you won't want to miss...

Other Aslett books you won't want to miss...

Other Aslett books you won't want to miss...

NEW FOR 2000:

TITLE	Retail	Qty	Amt
Clean in a Minute	$5.00		
Video Clean in a Minute	$12.95		
Cleaning Up for a Living	$16.99		
Clutter Free! Finally & Forever	$12.99		
Clutter's Last Stand	$12.99		
Construction Cleanup	$19.95		
Don Aslett's Stainbuster's Bible	$11.95		
Everything I Needed to Know…Barnyard	$9.95		
How to Be #1 With Your Boss	$9.99		
How to Handle 1,000 Things at Once	$12.99		
How to Have a 48-Hour Day	$12.99		
How to Upgrade & Motivate Your Crew	$19.95		
Is There Life After Housework?	$11.99		
Video Is There Life After Housework?	$19.95		
Keeping Work Simple	$9.95		
LOSE 200 LBS. THIS WEEKEND	$12.99		
Make Your House Do the Housework	$14.99		
NO TIME TO CLEAN!	$12.99		
Not for Packrats Only	$12.99		
Painting Without Fainting	$9.99		
Pet Clean-Up Made Easy	$12.99		
Professional Cleaner's Clip Art	$19.95		
Video Restroom Sanitation Includes Quiz Booklet	$69.95		
Speak Up	$12.99		
The Cleaning Encyclopedia	$16.95		
The Office Clutter Cure	$10.99		
The Pro. Cleaner's Handbook	$10.00		
Who Says It's A Woman's Job…	$5.95		
Wood Floor Care	$9.95		
500 Terrific Ideas for Cleaning Everything	$5.99		

VIDEOS:

Shipping: $3 for first book or video plus 75¢ for each additional.	Subtotal	
	Idaho res. add 5% Sales Tax	
	Shipping	
	TOTAL	

☐ Check enclosed ☐ Visa ☐ MasterCard ☐ Discover ☐ American Express

Mail your order to:
Don Aslett, PO Box 700, Pocatello ID 83204 Call toll free 888-748-3535

Card No. _____ Exp Date _____

Signature X _____

Ship to:
Your Name _____ Phone _____

Street Address _____

City ST Zip _____

200 7/00